Writing During the Apocalypse

Writing During the Apocalypse
Reflections on the Great Unraveling

Ed Simon

BLOOMSBURY ACADEMIC
NEW YORK • LONDON • OXFORD • NEW DELHI • SYDNEY

BLOOMSBURY ACADEMIC

Bloomsbury Publishing Inc, 1359 Broadway, New York, NY 10018, USA
Bloomsbury Publishing Plc, 50 Bedford Square, London, WC1B 3DP, UK
Bloomsbury Publishing Ireland, 29 Earlsfort Terrace, Dublin 2, D02 AY28, Ireland

BLOOMSBURY, BLOOMSBURY ACADEMIC and the Diana logo are
trademarks of Bloomsbury Publishing Plc

First published in the United States of America 2026

Copyright © Ed Simon, 2026

For legal purposes the Acknowledgments on p. xi constitute an extension of this copyright page.

Cover design by Daniel Benneworth-Gray
Cover image: Destruction by Thomas Cole (1836)

All rights reserved. No part of this publication may be: i) reproduced or transmitted in any form, electronic or mechanical, including photocopying, recording or by means of any information storage or retrieval system without prior permission in writing from the publishers; or ii) used or reproduced in any way for the training, development or operation of artificial intelligence (AI) technologies, including generative AI technologies. The rights holders expressly reserve this publication from the text and data mining exception as per Article 4(3) of the Digital Single Market Directive (EU) 2019/790.

Bloomsbury Publishing Inc does not have any control over, or responsibility for, any third-party websites referred to or in this book. All internet addresses given in this book were correct at the time of going to press. The author and publisher regret any inconvenience caused if addresses have changed or sites have ceased to exist, but can accept no responsibility for any such changes.

A catalogue record for this book is available from the British Library.

A catalog record for this book is available from the Library of Congress.

ISBN: HB: 979-8-7651-2322-5
        PB: 979-8-7651-2321-8
        ePDF: 979-8-7651-2324-9
        eBook: 979-8-7651-2323-2

Typeset by Integra Software Services Pvt. Ltd.
Printed and bound in the United States of America

For product safety related questions contact productsafety@bloomsbury.com.

To find out more about our authors and books visit www.bloomsbury.com and sign up for our newsletters.

"Depend upon it, Sir, when a man knows he is to be hanged in a fortnight, it concentrates his mind wonderfully."
—Dr. Johnson, as quoted in James Boswell's
Life of Samuel Johnson *(1791)*

Dedicated with love to Meg, my apocalypse buddy.

Contents

Acknowledgments xi

Introduction: A Syllabus on the End of the World; or, Meditations in an Extinction 1

Part One—White Horse 17

1. On Pandemic and Literature 19
2. Letter from the Pestilence—March 18, 2020 (Washington, D.C.) 31
3. Letter from the Other Shore—March 30, 2020 (Washington, D.C.) 37

Part Two—Red Horse 47

4. On War and Literature 49
5. Letter from Wartime—September 24, 2020 (Washington, D.C.) 65
6. Letter from the Capitol—January 14, 2021 (McLean, VA) 77

Part Three—Black Horse 87

7. On Technology and Literature 89
8. Letter from the Singularity—August 2, 2017 (New York City) 105

Part Four—A Pale Horse 121
9 On Literature and the Anthropocene 123
10 Letter from the Collapse—January 7, 2022 (McClean, VA) 153

Notes 166
Bibliography 187
Index 201

Acknowledgments

In addition to all of the scholars who've made this work possible and who are represented in the endnotes and bibliography, I'd like to make special mention of my colleagues in the English Department of Carnegie Mellon University. Thanks must go to Marian Aguiar, Jane Bernstein, Jon Klancher, Peggy Knapp, Jane McCafferty, Kathy Newman, David Shumway, Jeffrey Williams, Stephen Wittek, and James Wynn. In particular, special thanks among the faculty are due to Andreea Ritivoi, Christopher Warren, and Sharon Dilworth for imagining a space for the public humanities at CMU. I'd also be remiss to not mention editorial colleagues, including Adam Boretz, Sam Dresser, C. Max Magee, and Sophia Stewart. Finally, my eternal gratitude is for my family, my mother Janet and brother Jacob, and especially my wife Meg and my two boys, Finn and Milo.

Introduction: A Syllabus on the End of the World; or, Meditations in an Extinction

> *In times of crisis, we must decide again and again whom we love.*
>
> FRANK O'HARA, *MEDITATIONS IN AN EMERGENCY* (1957)

If you're both young and healthy with a life expectancy of several more decades, then you have a not unlikely chance that twenty, thirty, maybe forty years hence you will die in a flood or fire, a famine, or from some novel virus, in a refugee camp or drone attack from an authoritarian government. Abandon comforting fantasies of living into your ninth decade, expiring on your deathbed surrounded by loved ones, looking back on a life with few regrets while facing the unknown fearlessly. Much of the world already expects a violent demise for themselves; anyone reading this needs to also get used to that feeling. Armageddon has always been happening somewhere; as this century progresses, we'll just see apocalypse become globalized. If attuned to the recent changes in temperature—both figurative and literal—maybe you already have distressing premonitions about your fate, the fate of most of the people now reading this. Because on every major score—the political, the social, or the economic, Christ knows the environmental—the future will be worse than the recent past.

Ours is the era to have seen the resurgence of massive pandemics and violent ground wars, of increasing economic stratification and rising international authoritarianism, all of which harken to the most barbaric periods of the twentieth century, except our present is also dominated by the existential crisis of climate change. If epistemic doom is the tenor of our times, then the name of our age is the *apocalyptic present*, for this is an era in which regular definitions of past and future no longer hold, a moment in which one must look back to the Bronze Age collapse or the fall of the Western Roman Empire to find anything similar (and neither of those were marked by the same profound environmental changes we see today). Searching for a term to describe the current predicament, we can draw from the gravitas of grand rhetoric or the high-brow obscurations of academic jargon, but maybe it is far better to pick a term universally understood, and that is to say that we're collectively, irredeemably, and totally *fucked*. No better word encapsulates this moment.

If, for the past several decades, most who lived comfortably in what was at one time called the first world were able to ignore the signs of eventual civilizational and ecological collapse, the events of the previous decade have made such an incipient fate impossible to ignore now. Even while mass media and Western politicians obscured the true severity of our predicament, whether by false optimism or outright denial, the wider culture in literature, music, film, and so on has often been able to detect the faint vibrations of the four horsemen's hooves as they beat their way toward us from the darkening redness in the West. E. Ann Kaplan describes pop culture's prescience in *Climate Trauma: Foreseeing the Future in Dystopian Film and Fiction*, suggesting that "cultures may now be entering a new era in which pretrauma is pervasive in the public sphere. In this new era, media of all kinds—journalism, the Internet, television, film, and literature—offer catastrophic future scenarios."[1]

My own pretrauma was expressed during the time of Hurricane Sandy by listening to Arcade Fire's 2010 pre-apocalyptic album *The Suburbs*, for as Win Butler sang, "Even in the half-light / we can see that something's gotta give."[2] When that record came out, I was writing a dissertation about seventeenth-century apocalyptic narratives, but it was the melancholic lyrics on *The Suburbs* which spoke directly to what I was beginning to observe in that decade when the unravelling began to accelerate. Butler prophetically describes our "dead star collapsing," the sense that "something was ending." *The Suburbs* bears witness to the apocalyptic present by speaking of epistemic doom, our thrumming anxiety that remains just beneath the surface, felt by a multitude but frequently obscured by the official line. What I'm saying, in a roundabout way, is that the album made me feel less alone. "Though we knew this day would come," Butler sings, "Still it took us by surprise."

Because any fair and honest accounting of our current situation must lead to admitting that the world is dying, which demands a response from all of us, including the theorists and critics, artists and writers. That we're facing an apocalypse is clear not just to climatologists, but also to Cassandras in political science, epidemiology, computer science, philosophy, and most importantly, regular people who exist in the regular world and are witness to the reality that *something is happening*. In matters social, political, cultural, and especially environmental, there is an accurately felt deficit of optimism, a broad consensus that we're currently amid an unprecedented, existential, global crisis. On fronts political, economic, and environmental, we are barreling toward an abyss. All the threats we face are interrelated, bolstering each other and encouraging what so often feels like the inevitability of civilizational collapse. This is the "polycrisis," a term popularized by the British historian Adam Trooze who writes in a 2022 issue of the *Financial Times* that in the "polycrisis the shocks are disparate, but they interact so that the whole is even more overwhelming than the sum of the parts."[3] Economist Paul Krugman calls it the Great Unravelling in a 2003 collection of essays about the nascent George W. Bush administration.[4] Maybe it's a better turn of phrase than Krugman could have anticipated, because beyond the corruption, incompetence, and malice of the forty-third president's administration, "Great Unraveling" is a pithy description of our undeniable entropy, of the teleological slide into collapse whose signs are obvious. We are stalked by four horsemen, and their names are pandemic, authoritarianism, technocracy, and climate change. Their children are war, meaninglessness, and collapse.

For example, there has been the unmistakable global rise in far-right, if not fascistic, nationalism. Extremist political parties that are racist, xenophobic, misogynist, homophobic, Islamophobic, and antisemitic have governed in national offices as varied as Budapest and Brasilia; rightist political parties on all continents are following the template of Vladimir Putin's Moscow, with historian Timothy D. Snyder writing in *The Road to Unfreedom: Russia, Europe, America* that the last decade has seen a "rise of antidemocratic politics," manifested in phenomena such as the "Russian turn against Europe and invasion of Ukraine, the Brexit referendum, [and] the Trump election," all driven by the "stabilization of massive inequality, [and] the displacement of policy by propaganda."[5] The Washington, D.C., think tank Freedom House noted in a 2021 report that under a fifth of the world's population lives in a functioning democracy, with that being the fifteenth straight year of decline in democratic values both between and within individual countries.[6] Much of this turn toward totalitarianism will be further solidified in the coming decade through the intercession of increasingly sophisticated technologies, the era of surveillance capitalism ushering in a morass of memes and deep fakes, virtual reality, and artificial intelligence, all intended to bolster authoritarian politics.

During the summer of 2023, observers were shocked, delighted, and terrified by the borderline magical innovations in artificial intelligence, a field of computer science long considered at best moribund and at worst quackery. Now, ostensibly nonprofit corporations such as OpenAI have unveiled increasingly impressive AI engines such as Chat GPT 3 and its subsequently improved models, as well as other AI programs including DALL-E which is devoted to art, that were able to not only pass the Turing Test, but also write poems and full novels, produce realistic "photographs" of people who never existed or "paintings" in the style of any canonical artist on any subject which the person writing a prompt might request. Critics feared the coming emergence of not just a conscious machine but a type of inhuman superintelligence. The computer scientist Eliezer Yudkowsky at the Bankless podcast said, "that we are hearing the last winds start to blow, the fabric of reality start to fray."[7] Regarding the fruits of artificial intelligence, Yudkowsky said that "I'm not really seeing fifty [years] without some kind of civilizational catastrophe."

Maybe that's overly optimistic; perhaps our own planet will enact its revenge upon us long before our computers get a chance to. When it comes to resource depletion and anthropogenic ecological degradation, there are even more reasons to despair than there are when considering politics and technology. In examining several different interrelated "planetary boundaries," including climate change and ocean acidification, authors of a 2023 study published in the journal *Nature Sustainability* predicted "rapid destabilization of Earth's ecosystems,"[8] while two years earlier Corey J.A. Bradshaw writing in *Frontiers in Conservation Science* warned about a "ghastly future."[9] An indication of this ghastly future's shape is described in a 2023 article published in the journal *Current Biology* where the lead author, Yuangeng Huang, considers the Permian-Triassic mass extinction event of some 250 million years ago, the last time that the oceans had acidified and temperature had increased as rapidly as they have since the start of our own Industrial Revolution. Noting that we currently face a massive loss of biodiversity that most biologists now consider to be the planet's sixth great extinction, Huang writes that in "major catastrophes, a biodiversity crash may be the harbinger of a more devastating ecosystem collapse."[10]

Lead author Kumar P. Tripathy in an article from that same year in the *Proceedings of the National Academy of Sciences* warns about ecological "feedback loops," whereby increased carbon dioxide that raises the temperature can exponentially increase the overall greenhouse gas effects as substances like methane are released by melting glaciers, possibly making the halting of apocalyptic affects impossible. In their study, Tripathy emphasizes an attendant increase in erratic weather—droughts (and famines), floods, derechos, tornados, hurricanes, and wildfires—across the bulk of the planet's surface by the end of the century, something already clear to many in the summer of 2024, the hottest on record as of the writing of this book.[11] The Paris Agreement of 2015, signed by representatives of 195 nations, committed to a limit of an average temperature increase throughout the world of only 1.5 degrees above the pre-industrial average. Slightly more than that, writes David Wallace-Wells in *The Uninhabitable Earth: Life After Warming*, and the "ice sheets will be in their collapse, 400 million more people will suffer from water scarcity, major cities in the equatorial band of the planet will become unlivable, and even in the northern latitudes heat waves will kill thousands each summer." By 2032, we'll most likely have locked in an average increase that breaches the limits toothlessly placed by the Paris Agreement. Those results, horrifically, are "our best-case scenario," writes Wallace-Wells.[12]

Beyond the already apocalyptic nature of climate change, econometrician Gaya Herrington at *The Journal of Industrial Ecology* updated the parameters of an infamous 1972 investigation by MIT scientists, known as the "Club of Rome," who predicted civilizational collapse sometime in the twenty-first century. Examining variables including climate, but also population, fertility, and mortality rates; industrial output and food production; the depletion of non-renewable resources; industrial and agricultural output; persistent pollution; human effects on the environment; and overall human welfare, Harrington confirmed much of the earlier study's pessimistic conclusions, arguing that "continuing business as usual, that is, pursuing continuous growth, is not possible," while updating the likely date for widespread decline (if not the collapse) of industrial civilization being sometime around 2040.[13] This is not the flagellation of a Medieval millennialist or the haranguing of a sandwich-board-wearing street-preacher; such predictions are not made based on schizoid interpretations of Revelation or numerology rendered out of Daniel, rather they're rooted in a clear-eyed analytical reading of the empirical data. So all-encompassing and hard to envision is Herrington's contention—*that we're effectively less than two decades away from the collapse of industrial civilization*—that our powers of extrapolation fail.

This increasing alarm among many about the continued existence of civilization in some broadly recognizable form, not to mention the biodome of the planet itself, hasn't been exactly matched concurrently by a similar sense of alarm in the mass media, or even among most people—at least until recently. This hasn't just been a failure of policy writers and science popularizers either, because despite the emergence of "cli-fi" or "climate fiction" as a subset of speculative fiction, literary authors have by and large obscured the issue as well. Andrew Milner and J.R. Burgman in *Science Fiction and Climate Change: A Sociological Approach* discuss how in contrast to their subject, "'serious prose fiction' had become overwhelmingly committed to versions of literary realism that depend for their efficacy on notions of everyday probability," and so the subject of the Anthropocene appeared just too big to warrant expression.[14] Meanwhile, whether because of scientists' natural inclinations to eschew alarmist rhetoric or the inability of politicians to fully express the enormity of what we face, anecdotally, the attitude—even among those aware of the severity of our situation—is one of minimization, sublimation, denial. "A peculiar paradox became apparent in those years," writes Alexei Yurchak in *Everything Was Forever, Until It Was No More: The Last Soviet Generation*, "although the system's collapse was unimaginable before it began, it appeared unsurprising when it happened."[15]

Yurchak is writing about the period of Soviet history between de-Stalinization and perestroika, when an official cynicism became the state faith of most citizens who knew on the one hand that everything was in disarray, that the nation was on the verge of bankruptcy or collapse, but who functioned as if everything was fine, a phenomenon which the author calls "hypernormalization." It's an apt term for us, not the last Soviet generation, but maybe the last generation of humanity. We continue to work, to pay our bills, to keep up with our rent and mortgage and student loan payments, to pay taxes and plan for retirements that will never come. Even among those of us fully aware of the trends, that awareness of the score coexists with a fantasy that the future can continue onward as it always has in the past, though as the cynical online joke has it (always the most perceptive of artistic genres), even if the world is ending, you'll still have to come into work on Monday.

As with you, the reader, I'm simply a human during this particularly perilous time, and one who—hopefully also like you—has been attentive to the phenomena that endanger our continued existence, from the dogs of war in Eastern Europe, the Levant, and the South China Sea to the ever-increasing severity of Caribbean hurricanes and Pacific cyclones, of the ever-rising mercury that makes all subsequent summers the hottest ever recorded, even while I still go to work (or write this book). Central to Yurchak's understanding of hypernormalization is precisely this aspect, whereby it's clear that our own system is defunct, but it's also impossible to imagine any other way of doing things. In terms of the impossibility of imagination as a concept, hypernormalization bears some similarity to philosopher Mark Fisher's concept of "capitalist realism" in *Capitalist Realism: Is There No Alternative?*, in which that eponymous idea refers to our economic system's ability to preclude expansive and revolutionary means of even thinking of alternative ways of being, similar to Frederic Jameson's celebrated contention in a 2003 issue of the *New Left Review* that it's easier to envision the apocalypse than it is the end of capitalism.[16]

Hypernormalization is related to those arguments, but it connotes something a bit different as well, for while it's true that our ability to conceptualize an alternative way of being is precluded by the very systems under which we exist, it's also true that we're play-acting through the demise of that very same system whose rapidly approaching terminus all of us can anticipate, even if the end-date is presently unknown. There is a generational aspect to this malaise, one that I've anecdotally observed in almost two decades of teaching first-year undergraduates. At the beginning of my career, in the late days of the second Bush administration, my conservative students were animated by an annoyingly naïve and mythic Horatio Alger faith in the inevitability of their own personal wealth, while my more liberal students were later inspired by movements such as the (first) Barack Obama campaign and, after that, the #Occupy and the Bernie Sanders campaign, imagining that there was a preordained path toward an ever-progressive future. What happened instead was Trump and Covid-19, Ukraine and the Gaza invasion. Sometime during the last decade, belief in a better world—even if only for ourselves—seemed to wither for many people. At some point along the way, it was apocalypse that seemed inevitable—especially for ourselves.

Maybe it was that this shift in consciousness came with the "surprise" 2016 election of the demagogic fascist Donald Trump, or with the millions who died in that cruel year of 2020, or the strange weather of 2023 and 2024. Maybe it was with the unprecedented 2025 return of Trump, elected with a plurality (but not a majority) of voters, and thus dispelling any easy explanations for a cankered America's turn toward fascism. Disillusionment with bedrock beliefs is now widespread in the United States, if not the wider world, regardless of political orientation. (Arguably, a certain resigned nihilism is maybe all that we can agree on.) The arc of history, it would seem, bends toward annihilation. Because now our futures can be anticipated by the unseasonably warm days of a Northeastern winter or the record-breaking heatwaves of a Southern summer, with our eyes stinging from pollution generated from massive Canadian wildfires or the orange haze of a polluted sunset. One imagines that collapse will be a bit like Ernest Hemingway's barb about bankruptcy—that it happens slowly and then all at once. "We are only just entering our brave new world," writes Wallace-Wells, "one that collapses below us as soon as we set foot on it."[17] What our lot would appear to be is fires immolating Los Angeles and floods destroying lower Manhattan, of starving refugees fleeing Syria and Central America and fascist politicians in Europe and America answering that desperation with unspeakable violence, of crop failures followed by starvation and new pandemics. It remains to be seen if any newer and better phoenix will rise from the ashes of our rapidly dying world.

"I have made me a monument more lasting than bronze," wrote the Latin poet Horace in Ode 3.30 when considering the significance of literature.[18] This has often been a defense of the artistic life, the way in which literature bestows a certain immortality, but what sense does any of that make during the last generation? What possible utility could there be in organizing words as society crumbles and the planet collapses? If nobody is around to read your work, there is no impact to be had. Yet as philosopher Ben Ware argues in the journal *e-flux*, a "fight over language is a fight for an *unfucked* future."[19] The contours of our future—whether we can even have a future—must be imagined before anything else. To that end, this book is a modest entry in that venerable genre of *ars poetica*, an argument for the relevance of thinking, arguing, expressing, imagining, and writing during these hazy late days of the Anthropocene.

This will be accomplished by compiling separate syllabi for four different types of calamities—the epidemiological, militaristic, technological, and climatological—with the intent of demonstrating how women and men in the past have responded to similar contexts. Each of the four chapters is named after a respective horseman of the apocalypse as borrowed from the biblical book of Revelation, so that now the white horse refers to pandemics of disease, the red horse to militarism and authoritarianism, the black horse to unfettered technology, and that final pale horse to climate change, ecological devastation, and the Anthropocene. The first section of each chapter is dedicated to a theoretical, cultural, and literary analysis of a particular chapter's subject, while the second half of a chapter is dedicated to a personal consideration of that chapter's subject that was written while pertinent current events unfolded, as a kind of journalistic first draft of history. At the start of each one of these "letters," I indicate both its date of composition and the location in which it was written, the variety of the latter indicating some of the peripatetic nature of employment for a young scholar in this century. In his charming and perceptive *The Anthropocene Reviewed*, novelist Adam Greene explains that he "wanted to write about some of the small places where my small life runs into the large forces of the Anthropocene," and that's my own goal as well, to express a little of our apocalypse from my own limited perspective, hopefully elucidated through a critical understanding.[20]

Individual readings in each chapter's first section will focus on how given literary works grappled with said events. There are innumerable artists who explore what it feels like to live in this moment, a panoply of theorists who do the same. Drawing on all of those sources, my intent is to answer what possible purpose something like *literature* could have at the end of the world, for we continue onward, somehow, even though the glaciers are melting, the temperature is rising, and most of all our sense of reality is shifting with the fire being so close that the smoke stings our eyes. Apocalypse has always been a narrative, a story by which humans have ordered their experience and constructed meaning, even while the current data merges our most fevered prophetic fears with sober, empirical reality. Now, facing the sixth major extinction in our planetary history, which sees the largest die-off of individual species since the calamity that befell the dinosaurs 65 million years ago, it behooves us to ask what purpose stories even have. Since the fourth chapter of the book, "Pale Horse," considers our most pressing of challenges in the form of climate change, the first section of that chapter is further divided into four separate sections, each focusing more precisely on a purpose of writing (to whit, writing as memory, writing as protest, writing for meaning, and writing for preservation).

What I venture is that during the potential end of civilization, as we face the full extremity of an unprecedented polycrisis, there are four ways in which literature can respond and by which literature can be justified—to act as a form of resistance, a variety of witness, a method of preservation, and a way to generate meaning. Discrete, though necessarily overlapping, a unity to all those various functions of literature during collapse is one overriding purpose of reading and writing—that it provides a means to imagine alternatives to our current situation (even if only for the individual). With the parenthetical in the previous sentence, I've arguably already betrayed my promise to avoid the sentimental, yet I take it as a matter of faith that the shifting of consciousness can be as crucial as material change; that this isn't merely tending your own garden but the cultivation of the soul, a task infinitely more important and precious when we're all facing the executioner. This is what's so crucial about both literature and theory—its ability to force a reckoning and then to conceive of an alternative. As Amitav Ghosh notes in *The Great Derangement: Climate Change and the Unthinkable*, "the great, irreplaceable potentiality of fiction is that it makes possible the imagining of possibilities."[21]

Because my book is written from a subjective perspective about what it means to live and write during this particular historical juncture, it is by necessity even more individual and idiosyncratic than a conventional scholarly work would be. As much as this is a work of scholarship, it's maybe more a personal work by somebody trained in scholarship, marshalling the tools of theory and reference, quotation and research, to try and make sense of the current apocalyptic predicament in its collective implications and its personal effects. Calling autotheory a "pragmatic new form," Tasha Haines in *Redemptive Hybridism in Post-Postmodern Writing* describes how discursive, theoretically inflected memoir "has a ring of ingenuity about it—of composing terrain in a space where there is formerly none."[22] In that spirit, I'd suggest that any writing from *within* apocalypse must by necessity be in the first person if it's to be commensurate with its subject. Because what I want to convey is *urgency*, and a particularly *personal urgency* at that.

Such an approach is most obvious in my various "letters" throughout, these epistles being related to genres from personal essay to creative nonfiction, but perhaps because of the occasional theoretical jargon that is brought to bear, are most appropriately categorized as the public humanities. These letters need not be interpreted as taking part in the public humanities only because they attempt to use jargon in a manner accessible to a nonspecialist audience but also precisely because of their personal nature. Phillip Lewis in *The Public Humanities Turn: The University as an Instrument of Cultural Transformation* makes the personal nature of the discipline he's writing about clear, noting that many para-academic works must "set their reflections on the climate crisis in a highly personalized context," for what the humanities can offer at this moment is precisely this—*the human*.[23] As a caveat, however, this is a book by a relatively privileged American, so it is written from the perspective of an American (with all of the provincialism that implies), because apocalypse, like the future, doesn't happen everywhere at once. The apocalypse has happened many times before, it's happening in other places right now, and soon it will be happening here. It is to my contrition that my own perspective has limited my ability to fully grapple with those collapses that have already happened, that are happening currently.

Throughout *Writing During the Apocalypse* I will marshal those references that convey how irredeemably fucked we might be, but ultimately I take that reality as a matter of course; what I want to describe is the barometric drop that is hypernormalization, the widespread feeling of *epistemic doom* which I define as the sense among people that the world is ending, but with an uncertainty as to how and when exactly it will do so. That is the emotional tenor of our times—a spiritual tenor of our age. What is required, then, is this set of aforementioned syllabi for the end of the world. As such, each chapter (themed around Revelation's horseman) will focus on an aspect of our current collapse while being composed of a critical section and then a number of autotheoretical sections written as missives during the midst of particular historical events. As a work of personal cultural criticism, as a work of autotheory, what I intend to do in *Writing During the Apocalypse* is to not just make a series of observations about the polycrisis we're in the midst of (or maybe more accurately toward the end of), but rather to make a defense of the humanities—a defense of *writing*—when it seems that the world is ending. To do so by way of example and way of curation. I'm cognizant that such an *ars poetica* could easily degenerate into naval-gazing myopia, into the apolitical quietism content to tend a small plot of land which is the author's garden while the world burns. Even worse, in some ways, would be a retreat into gauzy, saccharine sentimentalism that proffers literature as balm, palliative, mere chicken soup for the doomed soul. As something *inspirational*. If I should accidentally court such a position—and perhaps it's inevitable—please show me forbearance. Perhaps by the time you read this book, the surprise of the end will have abated. If you're one of those people on the other shore, I wish you could let me know how we did.

Part One

White Horse

1

On Pandemic and Literature

There has always been literature of pandemic because there have always been pandemics. What marks the literature of plague, pestilence, and pandemic is a commitment to try and forge, if not some sense of explanation, then at least a sense of meaning out of the raw experience of panic, horror, and despair. Less than a century after the Black Death descended into Europe and killed 75 million people, as high as 60 percent of the population (90 percent in some places) all dead in the five years after 1347, an anonymous Alsatian engraver with the fantastic appellation of "Master of the Playing Cards" saw fit to depict St. Sebastian.[1] Making his name, literally, from the series of playing cards he produced at the moment when the pastime first became popular in Germany, the engraver decorated his suits with bears and wolves, lions and birds, flowers and green-men. The Master of Playing Cards' largest engraving, however, was the depiction of the unfortunate third-century martyr who suffered by order of the Emperor Diocletian. Even several generations after the worst of the Black Death, Sebastian's violent death still resonated with the populace, who remembered that "To many Europeans, the pestilence seemed to be the punishment of a wrathful Creator," as John Kelly notes in *The Great Mortality: An Intimate History of the Black Death, the Most Devastating Plague of all Time.*[2]

The cult of Sebastian had grown in the years between the Black Death and the engraving, and during that interim, the ancient martyr had become the patron saint of plague victims.[3] His suffering reminded people of their own lot—the sense that more hardship was inevitable, that the appearance of purpled buboes looked like arrows pulled from eviscerated flesh, and most of all the indiscrimination of which portion of bruised skin would be arrow-pierced, seeming as random as who should die from plague. Produced roughly around 1440, when any direct memory of the greatest bubonic plague had long since passed (even while smaller reoccurrences occurred for centuries), the Master of the Playing Cards presents a serene Sebastian, tied to a short tree while four archers pummel him with arrows.[4] Unlike more popular depictions of the saint, such as Andrea Mantegna's painting made only four decades later, or El Greco's and Peter Paul Reubens' explicitly lithe and beautiful Sebastians made in respectively the sixteenth and seventeenth centuries, the engraver gives us a calm, almost bemused, martyr. He has an accepting smile on his face. Two arrows protrude from his puckered flesh. More are clearly coming.

Sebastian didn't just become associated with the plague as a means of saintly intercession but also because, in his narrative, there was the possibility of metaphor to make sense of the senseless. Medical historian Roy Porter writes, in *Flesh in the Age of Reason: The Modern Foundations of Body and Soul*, that the "Black Death of the mid-fourteenth century and subsequent outbreaks ... had, of course, cast a long, dark shadow, and their aftermath was the culture of the Dance of Death, the worm-corrupted cadaver, the skull and crossbones and the charnel house."[5] All of said accoutrement, which endures even today from the cackling skulls of Halloween to the pirates' flag, serves to, if not make pandemic comprehensible, then at least to tame it a bit. Faced with calamity, this is what the stories told and the images made were intended to do, and religion supplied the largest storehouse of ready-made narrative with which to do this, even while the death toll increasingly made traditional belief untenable. For as John Hatcher writes in *The Black Death: A Personal History*, many lost "faith in their religion and ... [abandoned] themselves to fate," where fatality is as unpredictable as where an arrow will land.[6]

A different narrative, though not unrelated, was depicted forty years later. Made by the Swedish painter Albertus Pictor and applied to the white walls of the rustic Täby Church north of Stockholm, the mural presents what appears to be a wealthy merchant playing a (losing) game of chess against Death.[7] Skeletal and grinning, Death appears with the same boney twisted smile that is underneath the mask of every human face, the embodiment and reminder of everyone's ultimate destination. Famously the inspiration for director Ingmar Bergman's 1957 film *The Seventh Seal*, Pictor's picture is a haunting *memento Mori*, a very human evocation of the desperate flailing against the inevitable. Both pictures tell stories about the plague, about the lengths we'll go to survive. They convey how, during a pandemic, predictability disappears; they are narratives about the failure of narratives themselves. What both court are Brother Fate and his twin Sister Despair. The wages of fortune are the subject of which cards you're dealt, as well as the tension of strategy and luck when you avoid having your bishop or rook taken. Life may be a game, but none of us are master players, and sometimes we're dealt a very bad hand.

Narrative is an attempt to stave off meaninglessness and, in the void of the pandemic literature, serves the purpose of trying, however desperately, to stop the bleeding. It makes sense that the most famous literary work to come out of the plague is Giovanni Boccaccio's 1353 *The Decameron*, with its frame conceit of a hundred bawdy, hilarious, and erotic stories told by seven women and three men over ten days while they're quarantined in a Tuscan villa outside Florence.[8] As the pandemic rages through northern Italy, Boccaccio's characters distract themselves with funny, dirty stories, but the anxious intent from those young women and men self-exiled within cloistered walls is that "Every person born into this world has a natural right to sustain, preserve and defend" their own life, so that storytelling becomes its own palliative to drown out the howling of those dying on the other side of the ivy-covered stone walls.[9]

Pandemic literature exists not just to analyze the reasons for the pestilence—that may not even be its primary purpose. Rather, the telling of stories is a reminder that sense still exists somewhere, that if there is not meaning outside of the quarantine zone, there's at least meaning within our invented stories. Literature is a reclamation against that which illness represents—that the world is not our own. As the narrator of Albert Camus's 1947 *The Plague* says, as disease ravages the town of Oran in French Algeria, there is an "element of abstraction and unreality in misfortune. But when an abstraction starts to kill you, you have to get to work on it."[10] When confronted with the erraticism of etiology, the arbitrariness of infection, the randomness of illness, we must contend with the reality that we are not masters of this world. We have become such seeming lords of nature that we've altered the very climate, and geologists have named our epoch after humanity itself, and yet a cold virus can have more power than an army. Kate Rigby in *Dancing with Disaster: Environmental Histories, Narratives, and Ethics for Perilous Times* argues that "Epidemic disease is one kind of eco-catastrophe that brings us up hard and fast against the limits of hospitality," that is, against the limits of society, the limits of what it means to be a human.[11] As such, disease is not metaphor, symbol, or allegory, it is simply something which kills you without consideration. Story is a way of trying to impart a bit of that consideration which nature ignores.

The necessity of literature in the aftermath of pandemic is movingly illustrated in Emily St. John Mandel's 2014 novel *Station Eleven*. Mostly taking place several years after the "Georgia Flu" has killed the vast majority of humans on the planet and civilization has collapsed, Mandel's novel follows a troupe of Shakespearean actors as they travel by caravan across a scarred Great Lakes region on either side of the U.S.-Canadian border. "We bemoaned the impersonality of the modern world," Mandel writes, "but that was a lie."[12] *Station Eleven* is, in some sense, a love letter to a lost world, which is to say the world (currently) of the reader. Our existence "had never been impersonal at all," she writes, and the novel gives moving litanies of all that was lost in the narrative's apocalypse, from chlorinated swimming pools to the mindlessness of the internet. There is a tender love of every aspect of our stupid world, so that how the crisis happened can only be explained because of the fact that we were so interconnected. "There had always been a massive delicate infrastructure of people, all of them working unnoticed around us, and when people stop going to work, the entire operation grinds to a halt."[13] As survivors struggle to rebuild, it's the job of narrative to supply meaning to that which disease has taken away, or as the motto painted on the wagon of the traveling caravan has it: "Survival is insufficient."[14]

The need to tell stories, to use narrative to prove some continuity with a past obliterated by pandemic, is the motivating impulse of English professor James Smith, the main character in Jack London's largely forgotten 1912 post-apocalyptic novel *The Scarlet Plague*. With shades of Edgar Allan Poe, London imagines a 2013 outbreak of hemorrhagic fever called the "Red Death." Infectious, fast-moving, and fatal, the plague wipes out most of the world's population, so that some six decades after the pestilence first appears, Smith can scarcely believe that his memories of a once sophisticated civilization aren't illusions. Still, the former teacher is compelled to tell his grandchildren about the world before the Red Death, even if he sometimes imagines that they are lies. "The fleeting systems lapse like foam," writes London, "That's it—foam, and fleeting. All man's toil upon the planet was just so much foam."[15]

The Scarlet Plague ends in a distant 2073, the same year that Mary Shelley's 1826 forerunner of the pandemic novel, *The Last Man*, was set. Far less famous than Shelley's *Frankenstein*, this lesser-read novel is arguably just as pathbreaking, though partially anticipated by Jean-Baptiste Cousin de Grainville's fantasy of the same name from 1805. As with *Station Eleven*, narrative and textuality are the central concerns of the novel; when the last man himself notes that "I have selected a few books; the principal are Homer and Shakespeare—But the libraries of the world are thrown open to me," there is the sense that even in the finality of his position there is a way in which words can still define our reality, anemic though it may now be.[16] Displaying the trademark uneasiness about the idea of fictionality which often marked nineteenth-century novels, Shelley's conceit is that you're reading transcriptions of parchment containing ancient oracular predictions which the author herself discovered while exploring caves outside of Naples that had once housed the temple of the Cumae Sibylline.

Her main character is a masculinized *roman à clef* of Shelley, an aristocrat named Lionel Verney who lives through the emergence of a global pandemic in 2073 up through the beginning of the twenty-second century when he earns the titular status of the novel's title. All of Shelley's characters are stand-ins for her friends, the luminaries of the rapidly waning Romantic age; from Lord Byron who is transformed into Lord Randolph, a passionate if incompetent leader of England who bungles that nation's response to the pandemic, to her own husband Percy who becomes Adrian, the son of the previous king who has chosen to embrace republicanism. By the time Verney begins his solitary pilgrimage across a desolate world, with only the ghosts of Homer and Shakespeare and an Alpine sheepdog whom he adopts, he still speaks in a first person addressed to an audience of nobody. "Thus around the shores of deserted earth, while the sun is high, and the moon waxes or wanes, angels, the spirts of the dead, and the ever-open eye of the Supreme, will behold ... the LAST MAN."[17] Consequently, in a world devoid of people, Verney becomes the book and the inert world becomes the reader.

The Last Man's first-person narration, ostensibly directed to a world absent of people who could read it, belies a deeper reason for the existence of language than mere communication—to construct a world upon the ruins, to bear a type of witness, even if it's solitary. Language need not be for others; that it's for ourselves is often good enough. Literature thus becomes affirmation; more than that, it becomes rebellion, a means of saying within pandemic that we once existed, and that microbe and spirochete can't abolish our voices, even if bodies should wither. That's one of the most important formulations of Tony Kushner's magisterial 1991 play *Angels in America: A Gay Fantasia on National Themes*.[18] Arguably the most canonical text to emerge from the horror of the AIDS crisis, Kushner's three-hour play appears in two parts, "Millennium Approaches" and "Perestroika," and it intermixes two narrative threads, the story of wealthy WASP scion Prior Walter's HIV diagnosis and his subsequent abandonment by his scared lover Louis Ironson, and the arrival to New York City of the closeted Mormon Republican Joe Pitt who works as a law clerk and kindles an affair with Louis.

Angels in America combines subjects as varied as Jewish immigration in the early twentieth-century, kabalistic and Mormon cosmology (along with a baroque system of invented angels), the reprehensible record of the closeted red-baiting attorney and Joseph McCarthy acolyte Roy Cohn, the endurance of the gay community struggling against the AIDS epidemic and their activism opposing the quasi-genocidal non-policy of conservative politicians like Ronald Reagan. If all that sounds heady, Kushner's play came from the estimably pragmatic issue of how a community survives a plague. Born from the pathbreaking work of activist groups like ACT UP, *Angels in America* has an understanding that pandemics and politics are inextricably connected. In answering who deserves treatment and how such treatment will be allocated, we've already departed from the realm of disinterested nature. "There are no gods here, no ghosts and spirits in America, no spiritual past," says Louis, "there's only the political, and the decoys and the ploys to maneuver around the inescapable battle of politics."[19] Throughout *Angels in America*, there is an expression of the human tragedy of pandemic, the way that beautiful young people in the prime of life can be murdered by their own bodies. Even Cohn, that despicable quasi-fascist, who evidences so little of the human himself, is entitled to some tenderness when, upon his death, kaddish is recited for him—by the spirit of Ethel Rosenberg, the supposed Soviet spy in whose execution the lawyer was instrumental.

At the end of the play, Prior stands at Bethesda Fountain in Central Park, with all the attendant religious implications of that place's name, and he intones, "This disease will be the end of many of us, but not nearly all, and the dead will be commemorated and will struggle on with the living, and we are not going away. We won't die secret deaths anymore ... We will be citizens. The time has come."[20] In telling stories, there is not just a means of constructing meaning, or of even endurance, but indeed of survival. Fiction is not the only means of expressing this, of course, or even necessarily the most appropriate. Journalist Randy Shilts accomplished something similar to Kushner in his classic account *And the Band Played On: Politics, People, and the AIDS Epidemic*, which soberly, clinically, and objectively chronicled the initial outbreaks of the disease among the San Francisco gay community.[21]

In a manner not dissimilar to Daniel Defoe's classic *A Journal of the Plague Year, 1666* (even while that book is fictionalized), Shilts gives an epidemiological account of the numbers, letting the horror speak through science more effectively than had it been rendered in poetry. Such staidness is its own requirement, and can speak powerfully to the reality of the event, whereby "the unalterable tragedy at the heart of the AIDS epidemic" was that "By the time America paid attention to the disease, it was too late to do anything about it," the shame of a nation whereby Reagan's Press Secretary Larry Speakes would actually publicly laugh at the idea of a "gay plague."[22] Shilts waited till he finished *And the Band Played On* to be tested for HIV himself, worried that a positive diagnosis would alter his journalistic objectivity. He would die of AIDS-related complications in 1994, having borne witness to the initial years of the epidemic, abjuring the cruel inaction of government policy with the disinfectant of pure facts.

Most people who read about pandemics, however, turn to pulpier books; paperback airport novels like Michael Crichton's clinical fictionalized report about an interstellar virus *The Andromeda Strain*, Robin Cook's nightmare fuel about a California Ebola pandemic in *Outbreak*, and Stephen King's magisterial post-apocalyptic epic *The Stand*, which I read in the summer of 1994 and remains the longest sustained narrative I think I've ever engaged with. Because these books are printed on cheap paper and have the sorts of garish covers intended more for mass consumption than prestige, they're dismissed as prurient or exploitative. Ever the boring distinctions between genre and literary fiction, for though the pace of suspense may distinguish entertainment as being integral to the form's aesthetics, they too have just as much to say about the fear and experience of illness as do any number of explicitly more "serious" works.

The Stand is a pertinent example of just what genre fiction is capable of, especially when it comes to elemental fears surrounding plague which seem somehow encoded within our cultural DNA for more than seven centuries.[23] Written as an American corollary to J.R.R. Tolkien's *Lord of the Rings* trilogy, King depicts a United States completely unraveled one summer after the containment loss of a government "Super-Flu" bioweapon nicknamed "Captain Trips." In that aftermath, King presents a genuinely apocalyptic struggle between good and evil that's worthy of Revelation, but intrinsic to this tale of pestilence is the initial worry that accompanies a scratchy throat, watery eyes, a sniffling nose, and a cough that seemingly won't go away. If anything, King's vision is resolutely in that medieval tradition of fortune as so expertly represented by the Master of the Playing Cards or Pictor, a wisdom that when it comes to disease, "Life was such a wheel that no man could stand upon it for long. And it always, at the end, came round to the same place again."[24]

Far from being exploitative, of only offering readers the exquisite pleasure of vicariously imagining all of society going to complete shit, there is a radical empathy at the core of much genre fiction. Readers of Robert Kirkman, Tony Moore, and Charlie Adlard's graphic novels *The Walking Dead* (or the attendant television series), or viewers of George Romero's brilliant zombie classics, may assume that they'll always be the ones to survive Armageddon, but they can force us into a consideration of the profound contingency of our own lives. Cynics might say that the enjoyment derived from zombie narratives is that they provide a means of imagining that most potent of American fantasies—the ability to shoot your neighbor with no repercussions. More than that, however, I think that they state a bit of the feebleness of our civilization.

This is what critic Susan Sontag in *Illness as Metaphor* notes about how pandemic supplies "evidence of a world in which nothing important is regional, local, limited; in which everything that can circulate does, and every problem is, or is destined to become, worldwide," so that products and viruses alike can freely move in a globalized world.[25] The latter can then disrupt the former, where plague proves the precariousness of the supply lines that keep food on grocery shelves and electricity in the socket; the shockingly narrow band separating hot breakfast and cold beer from the nastiness, brutishness, and shortness of life is anarchic. Such is the grim knowledge of Max Brooks' *World War Z*, where "They teach you how to resist the enemy, how to protect your mind and spirit. They don't teach you how to resist your own people."[26]

If medieval art and literature embraced the idea of fate, whereby it's impossible to know who shall be first and who shall be last once the plague rats have entered port, then contemporary genre fiction has a similar democratic vision, a knowledge that wealth, power, and prestige can mean little after you've been coughed on. When the Black Death came to Europe, no class was spared; it took the sculptor Andrea Pisano and the banker Giovanni Villani, the painter Ambrogio Lorenzetti and the poet Jeuan Gethin, the mystic Richard Rolle and the philosopher William of Ockham, and the father, mother, and friends of Boccaccio. Plague upended society more than any revolution could, and there was a strange egalitarianism to the body-pit covered in lye. Sontag, again, writes that

> Illness is the night-side of life, a more onerous citizenship. Everyone who is born holds dual citizenship, in the kingdom of the well and in the kingdom of the sick. Although we all prefer to use only the good passport, sooner or later each of us is obliged, at least for a spell, to identify ourselves as citizens of that other place.[27]

Such equality motivated the greatest of medieval artistic themes to emerge from the Black Death, that of the *Danse Macabre* or "Dance of Death." In such imagery, painters and engravers would depict paupers and princes, popes and peasants, all linking hands with grinning brown skeletons that had hair clinging to mottled pates and cadaverous flesh hanging from bones, dancing in a circle across a bucolic countryside.[28] In the anonymous *Totentanz* of 1460, the narrator writes, "Emperor, your sword won't help you out / Scepter and crown are worthless here / I've taken you by the hand / For you must come to my dance." During the Black Death, the fearful and the denialists alike explained the disease as due to a confluence of astrological phenomenon or noxious miasma, they claimed it was punishment for sin, or they blamed religious and ethnic minorities within their midst. To some, the plague was better understood as "hoax" than reality. The smiling skulls of the *Danse Macabre* laugh at that sort of cowardly narcissism, for they know that pestilence is a feature of our reality and that reality has a way of collecting its debts.

Illness sees no social stratification—it comes for bishop and authoritarian theocrat, king and germophobic president alike. The final theme of the literature of pandemic, born from the awareness that this world is not ours alone, is that we can't avert our eyes from the truth, no matter how cankered and ugly it may be in the interim. Something can be both true and senseless. The presence of disease is evidence of that. When I was little, my grandma told me stories about when she was a girl during the 1918 Spanish Influenza epidemic that took 75 million people. She described how in front of the courthouse of her small Pennsylvania town wagons would arrive carting coffins for those who perished. Such memories are recounted to create meaning, to bear witness, to make sense, to warn, to exclaim that we were here, that we're still here. Narrative can preserve and remake the world as it falls apart. Such is the point of telling any story. Illness reminds us that the world isn't ours; literature lets us know that it is—sometimes.

Now—take stock. Be safe. Most of all, take care of each other. And wash your hands.

2

Letter from the Pestilence—March 18, 2020 (Washington, D.C.)

One particularly brutal winter, more than half a decade ago now, I used to find myself fantasizing about stripping down to my underwear and t-shirt and calmly walking out into the massive field of snow that blanketed the flat lot across from my apartment complex so that I could quietly freeze to death. These daydreams came on casually, and it was only after a few times of realizing that I had been online looking up "What does it feel like to die from the cold?" that I might be in trouble. For several weeks following an arctic blast, my small Pennsylvania town was covered in snow and ice, which the tax-averse city fathers did little to clear up. Though I obviously wasn't ensconced inside my apartment for the entirety of that time period, able to mostly slide down the hill to my job, and more frequently to the bar where I could get black-out drunk and somehow amazingly get back home, the isolation somehow felt both metaphorical and literal. During that time, I mostly kept company with box wine, liquor, beer, and a Netflix subscription, and despite my Google searches, I thankfully never saw fit to try my experiment during those blackouts. Weather wasn't the cause of my depression, obviously; my father was dying of a terminal illness at the time, I had yet to figure out that I should stop drinking, and there was some betrayal in my brain chemistry. But the chill permanence of the starkly beautiful and isolated landscape was certainly an affirmation of the pathetic fallacy, every bit as trite as if I'd made it up for a book. I eventually came out of the depression—as one does.

If you've ever been depressed, then you know the way in which sometimes it feels like you've been wearing dark sunglasses on a bright day; the strange film that seems to cover everything and muck up the synapses in your brain. There might be drama to some people's depression, and while there was certainly anxiety and the dull hiss of fear punctuated by moments of panic in mine, for much of it, there was a surprisingly low volume. It occupied me all the time, but there was something almost relaxed about it, how the way the moment before you freeze to death is supposed to feel as if a gentle letting go of one sense after the other. One of the signs of depression is that you lose interest in things which you love. In a clinical sense, that was true for me; I abandoned a lot of the intellectualization of literature that was my passion (and my paying job as a graduate student), but in a far deeper way, it wasn't accurate at all. Maybe I didn't want to write interpretations of poetry, teach the novels that I kept on teaching, or talk about drama in graduate seminars, but words were stripped to their most elemental and jagged nature for me, boiled down and rendered into a broth that I kept on drinking. This isn't going to be where I set up a false dichotomy between thinking and feeling, between interpretation and experience, nor is it a rejection of the critical discussion of literature. I truly derive pleasure from those things, and it was a blessing when my desire to engage them returned.

But when everything was stripped away from my desire, when I could scarcely feel love, least of all for myself, the words were still there. At the core of the humanities, it turns out, remains the human. Sometimes reading felt like running in place in a swimming pool; sometimes I was so distracted by my malady that the connection between sense and syntax was all but severed. I was lucky enough that I could still do it though, and with a dim awareness I understood that it was because I had no choice but to do so if I was going to come out of this on the other side. During this period, either ironically or appropriately, I read Andrew Solomon's stunning personal etiology, *The Noonday Demon: An Atlas of Depression*.[1] Much like Leslie Jamison's *The Recovering: Intoxication and Its Aftermath*, Solomon gives an account of our shared affliction from both history and medicine, as well as his own dark nights of the soul.[2] Solomon writes, "To give up the essential conflict between what we feel like doing and what we do, to end the dark moods that reflect that conflict and its difficulties—this is to give up what it is to be human, of what is good in human beings."[3] *The Noonday Demon*'s great power is that it doesn't reduce depression to character building, nor does it simply explain it away, but it does give some scaffolding of meaning to the experience of meaninglessness. Solomon's prose is exemplary, his empathy is complete, and though I don't personally know him, reading *The Noonday Demon* was just a connection enough, as weak as my transponders were, that a bit of static electricity was able to power me through when I got better.

I only bring this up because currently we're all in the pest house. What a strange thing, this social isolation, the self-quarantining? Suddenly, societal survival depends on all of us anointing ourselves as depressives, staying sequestered in our homes as whatever hell burns through the immune systems of our fellow humans. When I was depressed, I drew hope from the fact that other people weren't depressed; it felt like if my world was unravelling, there was at least a world. The surrealism of our current moment is that none of us have that same luxury anymore. Ironically, there's something democratic in our common situation, the way in which we're all feeling the same fear, the same uncertainty, the same panic, worry, anger, and anxiety. A solidarity, finally. If there's anything different from personal depression—and the sense of doom, the preoccupation with a malignant force, and the inability to fully immerse yourself in that which gives joy, that very much make this feel like a type of cultural depression—it's that there's also a weird joviality out there. The often very funny social media gallows humor (I'm partial to a picture of the advertising mascot Mr. Clean with the caption, "He left us when we needed him most") to the odd confessions with strangers, like the Trader Joe's checkout guy who told me he'd miss karaoke most of all.

The depressed, ironically, might have an immunological consciousness more prepared for this necessary quarantine. No longer kept in my apartment by diminished serotonin levels and several feet of snow, now it is rather the coronavirus that keeps me home. "Depression at its worst is the most horrifying loneliness," Solomon writes, "and from it I learned the value of intimacy."[4] Our school has been those feelings of nothing that have trained us in the art of that most human of things, our need for connection, precisely at the moment when it's necessary to sever those ties. "You cannot draw a depressed person out of their misery," Solomon correctly notes, but "You can, sometimes, manage to join someone in the place where he resides."[5] We live in an ugly era—mean, intemperate, cruel, cynical, narcissistic. Everyone says that of their age, but doesn't it feel a bit truer of our own? Now, as if the Earth has a breaking fever, it seems as if the very planet itself is shaking us off. We're all in that dark place now; some of us will get sick as well. Many of us will. We will all require kindness in that.

Just as Solomon's book was once something that I was able to hold onto, however so slightly, but which returned me to life, there must be an engagement with each other, with that which we've created, with that which exists to make connection, with that which joins us in the places where we reside. Creation can't be a luxury, nor is it just entertainment, or a way of passing time. Recently, I saw a video shared of an empty street in Florence, where women and men are quarantined in the city where once Boccaccio was sequestered from the plague, where Petrarch's beloved Laura de Nove succumbed to it. From an open window, a strong baritone voice from an unseen man starts singing in an Italian that I can't understand, then a woman joins in somewhere down the alley, then another man, then another.[6] Even the feral dogs in the street are barking joyfully by the end. All of them were isolated, but none were alone. Creation must be a kindness.

3

Letter from the Other Shore—March 30, 2020 (Washington, D.C.)

Beyond right and wrong there is a field. I'll meet you there.
– JALAL AD-DIN MUHAMMAD RUMI

They're constructing tent hospitals in Central Park across Fifth Avenue from Mount Sinai Hospital, and the foreboding is so palpable to me, the sense that for what's coming, there are scant preparations feels so visceral that I can barely stand to consider it.[1] New York used to be home, at least for the better part of most weeks when I'd commute in from small-town northeastern Pennsylvania to stay with my now wife while she was completing a residency in the city. Every decent person loves New York, and some indecent too, but that it stands as the greatest of American cities is so axiomatic that I care not to even make an argument on behalf of it. Central Park is the great lung of Manhattan; when my wife was at work, I'd wander the paths, the Ramble, the Great Meadow where now medics work. There are few places—for many of us—evocative of what a better world could look like. Think of it, unlike all those royal pleasure palaces in the world of old, Olmstead's lush urban garden is free and open to all. And now, the dying too. All I will say is that I've heard from those who still live in the city (for anyone in publishing knows a lot of New Yorkers) that right now the sirens are deafening, that there are refrigerated trucks parked outside the hospitals because of the morgue overflow, and that EMS is working longer and harder hours than they did during 9/11. Speaking of that seminal event which inaugurated adulthood for those of my generation (for that was a disquieting year to be an 18-year-old man)—sometime this week, our nation will begin to suffer deaths equivalent to the World Trade Center attack every single day until this burning stops.[2]

According to the almost certainly sugarcoated predictions of the man with the unenviable task of being the chief epidemiologist for our current, cankered administration, this pestilence could see 200,000 Americans die in the next few months—more than four times as many men who died in Vietnam.[3] If one consults the terrifying Imperial College of London report, the reality—if nothing was done and social distancing was ignored—would be closer to 2.2 million women and men.[4] That's more than twice as many Americans who died in the four years of the Civil War. After the rebels fired on Ft. Sumter, Washington, D.C.'s precarious position too many miles south of the Mason-Dixon Line made it an obvious target for Confederate invasion, so that President Abraham Lincoln ordered the capital to be heavily fortified, and in a few months, it became the most solidly protected city on Earth. Lincoln was not necessarily an optimist, but he was a hopeful man, and that is a difference. One thing that he wasn't was a denialist; when he refused to abandon Washington, he knew the score, capable of seeing from the balcony of the White House a massive Confederate flag flying from an Alexandria hotel across the Potomac, the pestilence already infecting the body politic, that symbol of secession leading to one of the earliest deaths of the war when an unlucky Union soldier attempted to remove the flag.⁵ Regardless of the city's fortifications, there were still incursions into the District of Columbia. The Battle of Fort Stevens, late in the war during 1864, resulted when Confederate Lt. Gen. Jubal Early invaded just over the northern border of the city from Maryland.⁶ When remembered at all, it's sometimes configured as just an unsuccessful scouting mission, but almost a thousand men died. The same number as the average losses we're about to suffer every day.⁷

Washington, D.C., is my home now; spring really is prettier here than it is further north, albeit it seems as if it is less earned after the warm winters. The cherry blossoms bloomed early this year; I gather they've been doing that more frequently as of late. I haven't been to the National Mall for a few weeks, even though it's less than a mile away. We're new to the city, so I still don't totally intuit that this is where I live; when boredom compels me to go for a brief drive, the neighborhood looking nothing so much like the bougie Mid-Atlantic neighborhood of my Pittsburgh upbringing, I'll occasionally turn one of those narrow, brick-lined rectilinear alphabet streets and suddenly see the Capitol dome. The experience always strikes me as strange and dreamlike, since I'd forgotten where I was for the past few weeks. All that dysfunction, all that callousness, all that refusal to see what we face while giving people the bandage of a one-time $1,200 check mere blocks from where I'm in quarantine.⁸

Not far from the site of Early's rebellious perfidy, and there's the National Arboretum maintained by the Department of Agriculture. Though a poor substitute for Central Park, the space is not without its charms, not least of which is the surreal spectacle of the National Capital Columns, an arrangement of twenty-two of the original Corinthian support columns from the United States Capitol, looking nothing so much like some abandoned temple in a field.⁹ They're uncanny, eerie, unsettling—like seeing the debris of a lost civilization that happens to be your own. A few weeks ago, before social isolation became de facto policy, my wife and her brother drove with me throughout the arboretum to see if we could enjoy any of the cherry blooms from my car window. The bonsai museum and the visitor's center were closed, but the paths were packed with people meandering in groups, as if nothing was different here, as if there was no need for fortifications at all, as if they couldn't hear Jubal Early moving in from the north.

The sirens are not yet deafening here, though I hear them more frequently. More medivacs flying low over Capitol Hill too. Whatever is coming is coming. It no longer feels like we're on the Potomac but waiting to cross the River Styx. I figure it might behoove me to gather some of my thoughts in an epistle here from the opposite bank of that river. Because I fear that none of us are prepared for what's coming; none of us can truly comprehend the enormity of the changes that will take place, even if some of us had our ears to the ground and could hear those hoofbeats coming months ago. Anyone who isn't an abject denialist, somebody enraptured by false paeans of positivity or an adherent of the death cult that currently masquerades as this nation's governing party can intuit the heat in the atmosphere, all that horror and sadness that's already happened, that's waiting to come. Those people dead in New York, around America, around the world. All those stories, all the narratives ended. If you've got your empathetic radio tuned into the frequencies that are coming out of every corner of the land, then the songs which you're hearing are in a minor key. Obituaries are starting to fill up with mentions of the virus, and those strange icons of celebrity have it—Prince Charles, Tom Hanks, and, most heartbreaking to me, the brilliant folkie John Prine. There's an unreality to the whole thing, as those seemingly unassailable of the rich and wealthy succumb to the pestilence. I wonder if it will soon seem more real to those blocking up the road in the arboretum?

Never forget that less than a week ago, several members of the chattering class of columnists who bolster the delusions, lies, and taunts of the junta were "simply considering" the possibility that it might be worth it to have a few million Americans die— the elderly, those with preexisting conditions, and a bunch of the unlucky among the rest of us—to jumpstart the economy.[10] As if an economy which demanded a blood sacrifice of citizens was an economy worth having. If we remember our villains after some of us have survived, then the pharaohs of the supply-side cult governing from the White House and the Senate should forever be emblazoned as a travesty whose intentions were a cruel pantomime of their self-described "pro-life" positions. Some commentators described them as offering the populace up as if infants to the Canaanite deity of bull-headed Moloch, who immolates the innocent in the fiery cauldron of his bronze stomach.[11] It'd be an overwrought metaphor if it wasn't precisely what was happening.

Anger is my most reliable emotion; I can convert sadness, depression, anxiety into its familiar and comfortable contours, so for at least a few hours of the day, I let myself feel that hatred toward the ghouls a few blocks down Pennsylvania Avenue. Otherwise, I'm like the rest of you, with little idea what soundtrack to put on as you rocket toward the singularity. I've no clue how one prepares for something like this, what one expects April, or May, or June to look like when you're facing that abyss that feels like the end of the world every day. Right now, I'm adhering to that old Program mantra of "One Day at a Time," and that seems to work while I'm white-knuckling it through the apocalypse. That means steadfastly following social distancing and getting proficient with disinfection. What one should also do, of course, is believe the science, believe in medicine, listen to the doctors and the epidemiologists who know what they're talking about (no matter how disturbing), and ignore the pundits, politicians, and talking heads who trade in masturbatory, sociopathic tweets while people die.

I'm under no illusions that what I'm doing right now contributes, for the best thing that all of us can do is to exile ourselves from this world. The woman I love more than my own heartbeat goes off to deal with this on the frontlines every day, so I know that anything I offer is paltry. Good Romantic that I am, I of course adhere to the power of words, the transcendence of poetry, the power to reach out and connect to others who are suffering. That's not just lip service, I do believe that, even while I think that washing your hands can be as immaculate as a poem, staying inside as triumphant as a novel. So, what I want to make clear is that right now I'm writing for myself and should any of that be useful to some of you, then I'm grateful. But I'm fundamentally offering a non-essential service, and it does no harm to my ego to admit that. What's difficult is to know what to turn to when facing something this unexpected, this enormous. Peruse Facebook and Twitter right now, there's a way of talking that's expected of late-stage capitalism, or post-modernity, or whatever the fuck we're supposed to call it. Snarky, outraged, absurd at times, perennially aggrieved, concerned with piffling bullshit. I suspect that by summer, many of us won't be talking that way anymore. I think, if we can, we should try and turn to something a bit more permanent, a bit more real, to help us hold our heads above water for a few more minutes, even while the water is burning our lungs.

In the coming weeks, the coming months, this whole damned year, there will be death. This will be a season of death. All of us will lose people we know, lose people that we love. The famous will die, and the unknown will too. Both the poor and the rich, the powerful and the powerless. Unless you were witness to atrocities in Syria and Iraq, unless you are a refugee from El Salvador or Honduras, or a survivor of when this government let young men die by the thousands simply because of whom they loved, little will prepare us for such staggering loss, I think. This devouring reminds me of a poem of crystalline beauty by the underread Irish poet Eavan Boland from 2008's *New Collected Poems*. In Boland's appropriately named "Quarantine" she writes, "the worst hour of the worst season / of the worst year of a whole people" during the Great Hunger in 1847, when the potato blight and its attendant famine decimated Ireland.[12] A million women and men dead, a million more forced into exile across the ocean. Victims of potato mold, yes, but more approximately humans killed by negligent or actively murderous government policy from the colonial rulers. Into that abyss, that cacophony of numbers and statistics, she reminds us that all of those millions were human beings, that each death was the conclusion of a unique story, placed into a mass grave and dusted over with soil.

Boland writes of "a man set out from the workhouse with his wife. / He was walking—they were both walking—north." Across this broken world, this scarred earth, Boland describes that the wife "was sick with famine fever and could not keep up. / He lifted her and put her on his back. / He walked like that west and west and north. / Until at nightfall under freezing stars they arrived." As a poet, Boland is no fabulist, she is no nostalgist, or sentimentalist. She does not give in to the charming narcotic of optimism and abides not by keeping spirits up. Boland is, however, resplendent with grace—in the full religious implications of that word. She writes, "Let no love poem ever come to this threshold. / There is no place here for the inexact / praise of the easy graces and sensuality of the body." Romanticism is a luxury that Boland can't countenance for her characters, not in Ireland, not in the black year of '47. This is a poem about "what they suffered. How they lived / And what there is between a man and a woman. / And in which darkness it can best be proved." She writes not of happy endings, but of the possibility, the reality of love. In her third stanza, the middle one, Boland writes:

In the morning they were both found dead.
Of cold. Of hunger. Of the toxins of a whole history.
But her feet were held against his breastbone.
The last heat of his flesh was his last gift to her.

What I'm saying to you is that I know not who among us shall live or die, but Christ, I pray that we all have the ability to be the breastbone.

I've decided to write an obituary for our dying world while I'm still well, while most of you are still well. The world is convulsing. I've no idea what it will ultimately look like, nor does anyone else, for that matter. Jeff Sharlet and Peter Manseau wrote about the aftermath of 9/11 in *Killing the Buddha: A Heretic's Bible*, asking, "How many times can the world end? How many times can it begin again? As often as you survive. As often as you tell the story. The apocalypse is always now, but so is the creation."[13] This seems right to me—the world is ending now. But something else is coming out of it. Possibly it could be a far worse world, the authoritarians and aspiring dictators using pandemic as an excuse to further tighten the noose, the obscenely wealthy retiring to their palaces as inequity grows even starker, and the people who bag our groceries forced into a virtual death sentence as disease runs rampant. Or, perhaps our current moment of unlikely solidarity, our new consciousness on what work is, what work requires, will continue unabated; maybe there will be a new demand of justice, new victories for equity, for fairness, for fundamental human dignity. In our current touchless epoch, it's impossible to know. All that can be offered is the breastbone, the reminder that you must give to those you love, even as the world ends.

I can list what I do know will be on that other side, what will be there after the world stops ending. Whenever we emerge, whenever we've buried our dead, whenever we've mourned the losses and tabulated the incalculable grief that we can barely comprehend in this darkest of Lents, I say to you that the following things shall be waiting: a plate of half-sour pickles at the Second Avenue Deli. The way Manhattan looks at sunset when first espied from a bus as it turns around the cliffs of Weehawken toward the tunnel. The perfumed scent of a magnolia tree at dawn. Primanti Brothers sandwiches. Calloused hands of strangers grasped together in a church basement as they utter the Serenity Prayer. Roadside rib festivals where flimsy napkins do literally nothing to sop the mess up as you eat. Corny and wonderful beachside art festivals where everything is pastel and painted on driftwood. Baseball (but the Pirates will sadly still suck). Dog parks where the concentrated joy is almost unimaginable. Refreshing summer breeze and spray rolling off the forks of the Ohio River. Scorching hot sand at the Singing Sands Beach in Manchester-by-the-Sea, and the attendant mystery meat hot dog purchased from a bored teenager. Ridiculously small-town music festivals where you can pay bottom dollar to hear classic rock warriors on their epic road downward, and yet they still absolutely shred it. Pittsburgh's skyline when you first emerge from that tunnel. Ice cream trucks. Cheesesteaks made with the worst meat but with the best of intentions. Cannoli. The Metropolitan Museum of Art's alabaster gleaming Roman room. The old men playing chess in Washington Square Park. Holding hands. Falling in love. The cherry blossoms. Central Park. The world on the other side of what's coming will not look exactly like this one. But there will be a world. I hope that most of us can meet there.

Part Two

Red Horse

4

On War and Literature

They make a wasteland, and they call it peace.
TACITUS, *AGRICOLA* (96 CE)

we (forgive us) / lived happily during the war.
ILYA KAMINSKY, *DEAF REPUBLIC* (2013)

While it is not the most wicked injustice of war, it is still a barbarity that so much of our attention is on the murderers and not the murdered. An argument can be made—good, valid, and true—that the names of those who started wars must stay on our lips as a curse, but let others do that, because I don't want to do it now. To focus only on the monsters is to reduce the innocent dead to corpses. Piles of rubble, of shoes and books and toys, of twisted bodies. We imperil our own conscience if we forget such evidence of life. Which is why I will not tell you the names of the two officers in the Japanese Imperial Army who, according to the *Tokyo Nichi Nichi Shimbun*, engaged in a contest to see who could first kill a hundred Chinese civilians during the invasion of Nanjing. According to the paper, one man had killed 106 innocent humans and the other 105, with "Both ... Lieutenants Going into Extra Innings."[1] I will not tell you the name of those two officers because I do not know the names of the 211 women, children, and men whom they murdered. I will not tell you the names of these lieutenants because I don't know the names of the 150 additional people they killed the following day. Such atrocities "did not penetrate the world consciousness," writes historian Iris Chang in *The Rape of Nanking: The Forgotten Holocaust of World War II*, "because the victims themselves had remained silent," and so I will not say the perpetrators names, for they had their own opportunity to speak at their trials.[2]

During the six weeks of invasion that started in December of 1937 some 200,000 Chinese civilians were murdered, with at least 20,000 incidences of rape (both numbers are likely lower than what really happened). Robert O. Wilson, an American physician in Nanjing, recorded in his diary that the "slaughter of civilians is appalling. I could go on for pages telling of cases of rape and brutality almost beyond belief," and he does, and if you need to read those, you can.[3] The doctor would testify at the International Military Tribunal for the Far East after the war's end; in 1948 that same commission executed the two who were involved in that horrific contest.[4] Whether or not it's good and righteous and just to execute those who commit such crimes, I do not know. As to if it's true or not that an eye for an eye makes the whole world blind, I have no real opinion. To take any human life makes me uneasy, but I will tell you that deep in my heart, I do not mourn for those two officers on the gallows, nor does the thought of them in Hell bother me, and whatever that says about me is something that I probably should have more concern about. I know that atrocities are committed by normal people, that those two may have grown up in loving families, that they may have delighted in their wives and children. I know that these soldiers were not demons, but that they were humans, and that that is all the more terrifying.

"Almost all people have this potential for evil, which would be unleashed only under certain dangerous social circumstances,"

Chang said in an interview.⁵ Also, important to remember that if everybody is capable of atrocity, only a small percentage of humans actually commit them, lest we obscure evil in the gauzy miasma of moral universalism. Yet the question of what drives men to such wickedness is forever unanswerable. Why are some Adolph Eichmann and Josef Mengele and by contrast others are Mahatma Gandhi or Oscar Romero? Chang's research involved discovering the involvement of German businessman John Rabe who established the Nanking Safety Zone, where through diplomatic immunity he was able to protect civilians and saved 200,000 people. Rabe was also a dedicated member of the Nazi Party.⁶ The only thing more mysterious than human beings is grace, whatever the origin of that grace might be. Separate from historical scholarship, intelligence reports, and national security briefings, war literature exists to comprehend the arbitrary nature of grace and damnation. If war literature is written to impart meaning, then all war literature is a failure. Nothing is so incomprehensible as war; not logistics, or strategy, battles for land, glory, riches, or liberation, all of which can be perfectly logical, but the *actual act of war*, of waking up knowing that your life could be taken or that you must take a life. We're told this is our animal nature, but the organized barbarity at Andersonville, or Dachau, or Nanjing has no corollary in the natural world. War literature exists not to impart meaning, but the appearance of it, so as to gesture at something beyond this veil of shadows. Something unutterable, and ineffable, and silent, and strange. War literature, at its best, exists not as scripture but as liturgy, not to explain but to remember. Chang writes that "to forget a Holocaust is to kill twice," and such writing ensures that we don't become complicit.⁷

Literature replaces the aridness of numbers with the texture of humanity, while somehow grappling with the full scope of an atrocity. When Joseph Stalin was Commissar of Munitions during the enforced famine known as the Holodomor, which killed almost 4 million Ukrainians in the mid-30s, he told a group of his colleagues that "If only one man dies of hunger, that is a tragedy. If millions die, that's only statistics."[8] What is grotesque is that this ruthless theorist of the human abyss was correct. When death tolls mount from the hundreds to the thousands, to the millions, the brain is only capable of processing so much. This loss has ethical implications, however, for who would be forgotten are victims like Myshko Cherkasy, a child who, when he died and was to be buried his mother discovered his grave already had another murdered child buried within it; Michael Kovrak who starved to death in front of his young brother; Olya Sturko forced to give birth upon the wheat fields at a collective farm, the mother ultimately perishing because of the shock to her system when she finally received a meagre portion of food after weeks of starving.[9] Journalist Petro Shovkovytsia wrote in 1933 how, to the Soviets, "These were not people, but rather shadows of people. Cut them with the dullest of knives, and you will not get blood to flow from them: beaten, tortured, exhausted."[10] The task of war literature is to transform shadows into pictures, to put flesh upon the bones of mere statistics. To square individual tragedy with the horror of mass atrocity, to mathematically transform the number one into an infinity. Ethically, the writer and their reader must *attempt* to comprehend that each singular murder is but 1 of 4 million. With one, or two, or three deaths in mind we must try and imagine all of the deaths. Holding to particularity, we must mourn for the multiplicity. That this is by definition impossible does not occlude our responsibility; if anything, it's all the more imperative. What is asked of us is something theological, to grasp toward the enormity of all that which we are incapable of understanding.

Every human is a universe; each individual in victory and defeat, love and hatred, desire and revulsion, is more complicated than all great literature, more beautiful than every painting, truer than all of the axioms of philosophy. The human soul is inviolate, and in its own flawed way, a species of perfection. Which is why murder is a sin, and to take millions of lives is a crime against humanity. Arguing that every human is valuable, that we're all equal, that all deserve dignity, security, safety, happiness, love. Rank schmaltz, right? Sentimental affectation, correct? *Cliché*. Ah, but here's the thing with genuine war literature—the ethical imperative is to understand that cliché is not the antithesis of truth. Another cliché—it might be hackneyed to say that it's impossible to explain war to a child, but that's only because it's impossible to explain war. "The violence of war is random," writes journalist Chris Hedges in *War is a Force that Gives us Meaning*. "It does not make sense. And many of those who struggle with loss also struggle with the knowledge that the loss was futile and unnecessary."[11] War literature which does something as sacrilegious as to *make sense* scarcely deserves to be called literature. Reduced to its basest formulation, war is the practice of resolving disagreements, or acquiring land, or erasing humans whom you hate by organizing men with weapons who then kill people until everyone is tired of all the killing, or everyone's dead. That is irrational, stupid, inexplicable, there is no making sense of that and so any honest war literature doesn't concern itself with such theodicies. "When meaning is drawn from killing," notes historian Timothy Snyder in *Bloodlands: Europe between Hitler and Stalin*, "the risk is that more killing would bring more meaning."[12]

A risk in reducing gun and wound to axiom and postulate, bullet to arid argument. You can't summarize a null point of meaning with anything as quotidian as a syllogism. That shining and polished blackjack-booted Prussian General Carl von Clausewitz claimed in *On War* that "War is a continuation of politics by other means."[13] Though perhaps the opposite is often just as true. I wouldn't deign to impugn von Clausewitz's instilling of bravery, loyalty, and respect within his troops, of inspecting ammunition and armories, of evaluating the Cannae model of troop formation in imitation of Hannibal's victory during the Second Punic War; but give me rather that grizzled frontiersman General William Tecumseh Sherman's opinion as he marched all the way to Savannah that "War is hell."[14] Those three words seem at least truthful. War isn't just hell, of course. War is also strategy, war is distraction, war is horror, war is entertainment, war is propaganda, war is spontaneous, war is planned, war is boring, war is exciting, war is oppressive, war is liberatory, war is wasteful, war is necessary, but most of all war is meaningless. At least the actual pulling of the trigger is. Being able to kill a man, the unawareness of if you'll return, the knowledge you may never see your family again, the reality that somebody else might never see theirs again because of you—all of that can't quite be circumscribed by logic or poetry. All war literature must be failed literature because it gestures to where words themselves fail. Such writing tries to express the inexpressible, for the moment that a human takes the life of another, language has already broken down. I'm not saying that historians shouldn't investigate the causes of wars, of course not, for the better to prevent them. But the actual *act* of taking a rifle and from a distance shooting a stranger in the head—that is madness. If logic comes out of war, then war itself is built upon a million illogical acts.

All honest war literature is fundamentally anti-war. That's not the same as saying that all war literature must be *pacifistic*. Kurt Vonnegut's auto-fiction/science fiction account of the Allied firebombing of Dresden in *Slaughterhouse-Five*, Norman Mailer's indulgent but trenchant *The Naked and the Dead*, Joseph Heller's hilarious and terrifying *Catch-22*, Dalton Trumbo's disturbing account of being caged within one's own destroyed body in *Johnny Got His Gun*, the German writer Erich Maria Remarque's exquisite account of World War I trench fighting in *All Quiet on the Western Front*, each and every one exemplars, each and every one anti-war, each and every one pacifistic, and tellingly each and every one by a veteran. Remarque explained that his book was to be "neither an accusation nor a confession, and least of all an adventure, for death is not an adventure to those who stand face to face with it."[15] But great war literature need not be pacifistic, only anti-war, which is to say that it comprehends barbarity. Two of the most poignant, brutal, and under-heralded war novels of mid-twentieth-century are Martin Booth's horrific *Hiroshima Joe* and John Horne Burns' *The Gallery*. Both books concern the ostensible "Good War" against the Axis Powers, with Booth focusing on the war against Japan, and Burns' writing about the occupation of Naples by the Americans. And both, while not arguing against the reasons for the war, focus on brutality enacted against "enemy" civilians, how innocence is never a quality of those who fight, regardless of their side's righteousness.

The titular character of *Hiroshima Joe* is Captain John Sandingham, a British POW captured by the Japanese in Hong Kong and witness to the unspeakable horror of the atom bomb. Sandingham observes the incineration of whole city blocks, women and men turned to ash, shadows burnt into sidewalks, and children with skin hanging from their bodies; he sees "what no man should be made to see, he died fearing what we all must fear," a world where there is no distinction between soldier and civilian, where peace itself is conquered.[16] *The Gallery* also disavows Manichean platitudes in fictionalized vignettes based on the American occupation of Burns' beloved Naples, where the ostensible good guys were involved in extortion, racketeering, rape, murder. Burns' novel is a warning at the dawn of the true American century, that "unless we made some attempt to realize that everyone in the world isn't American, and that not everything American is good, we'll all perish together."[17] An irony is that some of the greatest anti-war literature comes from the Second World War, arguably the most morally unassailable battle in human history. A generation after the Great War, and the "combatants were unillusioned from the start," writes editor Sebastian Faulks in the introduction to *The Vintage Book of War Fiction*. "They knew how gruesome war would be, they knew that they had been dropped into it by inept politicians, but in place of innocent patriotism of their fathers they had a proper moral cause to fight for."[18] If war is necessary, there's still nothing glorious about it. Between country or what's right, at the very least there's something to be said for fighting on behalf of the latter. As for myself, having never been anywhere near a frontline, a trench, or an active battlefield, I'm not a pacifist—merely a coward. There's a difference there as well.

In a war of defense or liberation there can be many things—loyalty and courage, honor and fraternity. Glory, however, is invented by poets. War is blood congealing on the dead grass at Flanders Field and brains sprayed across Omaha Beach, it's a gangrenous foot being sawed off at Manassas and bits of flesh dotting Hill 488. "I sing of arms," as Virgil begins *The Aeneid*, a topic of utmost seriousness since a man first struck another man, our story of creation not in Eden but when Cain slew Abel.[19] Triumph of kings and victory of the nation, glory of soldiers and the shame of the vanquished. Virgil's epic is great poetry, but it's also propaganda, albeit with its own anti-war moments studded like land mines within. The most antique of war literature, even when written to valorize, still has within it the seeds of truth. *The Iliad* of Homer, whether he had experienced war himself, is the great martial epic of valor, and yet within its opening lines there is the honesty which compels him to describe war as "Black and murderous ... Incalculable pain, pitched countless souls ... bodies to rot as feasts / For dogs and birds."[20] Achilles and Jason, Aeneas and Pallas, may fight with shields and spears, swords and helmets, while today soldiers wear Flak Jacket and brandish M4s, but the same absurd goal is at play—

kill the other guy before you get killed. Despite the social Darwinian fallacy that understands people as living in a barely contained state of nature, just three days' worth of good meals away from total anarchy, to kill a man is a supremely unnatural thing, especially a stranger, particularly one who has done nothing to you.

When humanists extol the canon's universalism, they reduce and flatten our differences with the past, and the reality is that we neither love, pray, live, or work like our ancestors in Rome, or Greece, or Babylon, but the score of being made to kill a man—and the resulting wounds—remains similar. That's the principle behind artistic director Bryan Doerries' Theater of War Productions, which stages readings of Greek tragedies like Sophocles' *Ajax* and *Philoctetes* for audiences of veterans as a way of coping with trauma. According to Doerries in *The Theater of War: What Ancient Tragedies Can Teach Us Today*, he has discovered that "people who have come into contact with death, who have faced the darkest aspects of our humanity, who have loved and lost, and who know the meaning of sacrifice, seem to have little trouble relating to these ancient plays. These tragedies are their stories."[21] English professor Elizabeth D. Samet has explored something similar in her teaching U.S. Army cadets among the bucolic red, orange, and brown trees of autumnal West Point. Reading Homer and Virgil, not to mention Ernest Hemingway's *For Whom the Bell Tolls* and Tim O'Brien's *The Things They Carried*, in a graduate seminar is one thing; teaching it to young women and men who are destined to one day experience such violence requires a different perspective. In her memoir *Soldier's Heart: Reading Literature Through Peace and War at West Point*, Samet writes, "We surrendered rather easily to yet another romantic notion: that meaning is to be found only in misery."[22] Surprisingly neither Doerries nor Samet read or teach war literature as involving spangled glory; the former emphasizes that playwrights such as Sophocles were not authors of morale-boosting propaganda, while the former's contention makes the radical claim that suffering isn't about meaning, that to the contrary it can often be about nothing. And yet suffering must still be endured, and so literature acts not to explain the inexplicable but rather to soothe, to say, "*You are not alone, this has happened before, this will happen again, not everybody survives but some people do.*"

"'Forward, the Light Brigade! / Charge for the guns!' he said: / Into the valley of Death / Rode the six hundred," wrote Alfred Lord Tennyson in 1854, mere days after the routing of the 4th and 13th Light Dragoons, 17th Lancers, and 8th and 11th Hussars during the Crimean War.[23] Few poets seem stuffier than Tennyson; patriotic, formal, traditional, and conservative, his verse ponderously Victorian while across the Atlantic Walt Whitman was breaking meter and Emily Dickinson was reinventing metaphor. All those exclamation points, that equestrian rhythm, that sickly celebration of valor. Yet even Tennyson drew a distinction between the incompetent men who sent boys to their death, and the boys themselves who "Storm'd at with shot and shell, / Boldly they rode and well, / Into the jaws of Death, / Into the mouth of Hell." This, it could be observed, is still mythological language, Tennyson describing the campaign in the language of harrowing. He chose the wrong genre, for war literature isn't myth, it's horror. What's lacking in Tennyson is the physical experience of war; he describes "Cannon to right of them, / Cannon to left of them, / Cannon behind them ... While horse and hero fell, / They that had fought so well."[24] This is basically a boy's fantasy of war. Tennyson might as well be describing soccer. The Poet Laureate wasn't a veteran, and it shows; it's what allows him to ask "When can their glory fade? / O the wild charge they made! / All the world wonder'd. / Honor the charge they made! / Honor the Light Brigade!" Now all that's remembered is a poem more pablum than Parnassus, each of those dead soldiers forgotten other than for some cenotaphs and memorials in England. What's missing is blood—gouged eyes—protruding bones—first-degree burns—festering bullet wounds—severed hands and crushed bodies. What's missing is the sense that death isn't metaphor or simile or allegory, but that death is just death, a violent one even more so.

Compare Tennyson's verse to Whitman's "The Wound-dresser" from his collection of Civil War lyrics *Drum-Taps*. Of Quaker pacifist stock, though a vociferous supporter of the Union, Whitman left Brooklyn for Washington, D.C., after hearing of his brother's wounding at Antietam, deciding to stay in the capital where he worked as a nurse in war hospitals. The good, grey poet would tenderly minister to the beautiful boys of American death, wrapping their burns and cuts, setting their broken legs, distributing sweets and occasionally reading his verse to men who undoubtedly had no idea that he was the greatest of American poets. "Bearing the bandages, water and sponge, / Straight and swift to my wounded I go, / Where they lie on the ground after the battle brought in, / Where their priceless blood reddens the grass, the ground."[25] Whitman is an abolitionist who comprehends that the Confederacy is defeated at Gettysburg and Antietam and nowhere else, but he is not delusional about the cost. Tennyson's Dragoons, Lancets, and Hussars are heroes, whereas Whitman asks in a parenthetical "(was one side so brave? the other was equally brave)." The British poem lacks blood, it lacks corpses, it lacks bodies, replacing them with abstractions. In "The Wound-dresser," Whitman describes "stump of the arm, the amputated hand … the clotted lint … the matter and blood." Whether or not a war is just or justified, righteous or right, Whitman understands that it results in men like the soldier whose "eyes are closed, his face is pale, he dares not look on the bloody stump, / And has not yet look'd on it." The difference between the poems is that Tennyson described war in terms of glory, and Whitman knows that it's about "clotted rags and blood, emptied, and fill'd again." One poem works because it tells the truth, and the other one doesn't work because it lies. As Remarque writes in the following century, "A hospital alone shows what war is."[26]

Besides, meter, rhythm, and rhyme can be useful, for what war lyrics are more successful than that of Wilfred Owen's and Siegfried Sassoon's accounts of trench warfare written during the Great War itself? Owen was a working-class Shropshire lad tutored on Keats, Shelley, and Yeats; Sassoon was from a wealthy Baghdadi Jewish family and was educated at Cambridge. The two read and admired each other, and served at the same time along the crooked, burning gash of the Western Front. As inheritors of a classical English education, both men wrote in a cadence that owes more to the measured traditionalism of Tennyson than the barbaric yawp of Whitman, and yet when war's madness can be barely constrained by formalism, its horrors are even more pronounced. "Soldiers are citizens of death's grey land," wrote Sassoon in *The Counter-Attack and Other Poems*, "Drawing no dividend from time's to-morrows."[27] Almost oracular, but the eloquence of Sassoon's rhetoric belies the horror it describes. From Owen's most famous poem, "Dulce et Decorum Est," written in the trenches themselves, he describes watching the burning, disintegrating, acrid death that results when a soldier is hit with mustard gas, for "someone still was yelling out and stumbling, / And flound'ring like a man in fire or lime … / Dim, through the misty panes and thick green light, / As under a green sea, I saw him drowning."[28]

The Great War surprised the great powers, doddering men who'd amassed massive armies and let their technology outstrip their empathy. A war fought between the first cousins who ruled Britain, Germany, and Russia, offering up as sacrifice millions of young men cooked in mustard and shot at by gatling gun on the barbed wire of broken Europe. Critic Paul Fussell, himself a veteran of World War II, notes in *The Great War and Modern Memory* that "Every war is ironic because every war is worse than expected," and the impact of Sassoon and especially Owen's verse is that it exists between the grandiosity of Victorian youth trained on myths of the Light Brigade when compared to the reality of Verdun, Somme, and Gallipoli.[29] When Owen describes the dying man's "every jolt, the blood ... gargling from the froth-corrupted lungs, / Obscene as cancer, bitter as the cud / Of vile, incurable soles on innocent tongues," he writes in an idiom that at the literal level of sounds is *beautiful*. Go ahead, read that bit out loud to yourself, listen to the cadence, the relationship of syllables to each other, the meter, the unforced rhyming, and admit that Owen has used beautiful language to describe an atrocity. And in that ironic gap, valor is erased by degradation. Owen expresses more about battle than propagandists ever could. He would die in 1918 while crossing the Sambre-Oise Canal. His mother received the telegram on Armistice Day, when bells were ringing in celebration throughout Shrewsbury.[30] "The old lie: *Dulce et Decorum Est / Pro Patria mori.*" Who knows what poems have been interrupted by a bullet, what novels disrupted by mortar attack?

Some of the surviving lyrics are assembled in Lorrie Goldensohn's remarkable *American War Poetry*, the first collection of its kind, including verse from colonial wars through Afghanistan, with sections dedicated to overlooked conflicts including the Spanish American War, the Indian Wars, and even the Spanish Civil War.[31] Goldensohn writes that poetry is a way of conveying "battlefield advance and retreat, the daring and courage of leaders and men, as well as the despoliation of territory, the experience of prison camp and the making of refugees, the annihilation and wounding of human flesh, the grieving aftermath."[32] Every emotion is expressed in such verse, from cruel jingoism to fear, from patriotic loyalty to absurdity.

Sarah Teasdale considers not the artillery of the Great War, but the silence which follows, for "There will come soft rains and the smell of the ground ... And Spring herself, when she woke at dawn, / Would scarcely know that we were gone."[33] James Dickey, American Poet Laureate and veteran of the Second World War, gives a meditation in incendiary and gasoline, writing of how "All families lie together, though some are burned alive."[34] Rolando Hinojosa recalls American atrocities during the Korean War, how "I don't want to look at the Chinese dead. / There are hundreds of them out there. They died in the city, / They died in the fields and in the hillsides. / They died everywhere."[35] Yusef Komunyakaa presents the haunting experience of searching for the names of dead friends on the Vietnam Veterans Memorial, where "My black face fades, / hiding inside the black granite."[36] For sheer, methodical, scientific accuracy, however, there is Iraq War veteran Brian Turner's masterpiece from *Here, Bullet* which provides both autopsy report and psychological evaluation. "If a body is what you want, / then here is bone and gristle and flesh."[37] That is what war poetry must be about, "where the world ends, every time."

If war requires any genre, it's not drama, or novel, or poetry, but journalism, bearing witness as to what actually happens when troops cross a border or bullet pierces flesh. Studs Terkel's interviews in *The Good War*, Philip Gourevitch's harrowing *We Regret to Inform You That Tomorrow We Will Be Killed with Our Families* about Rwanda, Aleksander Hemon's evocation of a Sarajevo youth before the wars in *The Book of My Lives*. Anthony Swofford expresses dark truths in *Jarhead*, his account of the Marine Corp during the Persian Gulf Invasion, and the fact that "as a young man raised on the films of the Vietnam War, I want ammunition and alcohol and dope, I want to screw some whores and kill some Iraqi motherfuckers."[38] Waiting for the invasion to begin, the bored Marines sit in the Kuwaiti desert and watch movies about an earlier confrontation. Francis Ford Coppola's

Apocalypse Now, Oliver Stone's *Platoon*, Stanley Kubrick's *Full Metal Jacket*. Swofford is blunt—all those movies might ostensibly be anti-war, but for the grunts trying to psyche themselves up listening to Wagner's *Ride of the Valkyries* as U.S. helicopters drop napalm, *Apocalypse Now* doesn't engender pacifism so much as adrenaline. Which is the corollary to all war literature being anti-war, and that's that war literature can't help but be prurient, exploitative, exhibitionistic, pornographic. The moment editing and revision happen, then you've made literature, a polite way of saying something with an agenda, and anything with an agenda is incapable of examining the unvarnished totality of anything, especially a black hole like war. True literature of war has never been written. It might not even be possible.

There's been some elision between violence and war in this essay. A sloppiness in that, because all war might be murder, but not all murder is war. Cain killed Abel, by himself. No general directed him. Violence might be natural (though so is cholera), but war is strange. "If wars were fought only be the men on the ground, the men facing one another in real battle, most wars would end quickly and sensibly," notes Swofford. "Men are smart and men are animals, in that they don't want to die so simply for so little." Often war is presented as a bestial return to a state of nature, but it's the exact opposite. With few exceptions, animals don't engage in war, though they kill each other all the time. War is not the daughter of nature, but rather the son of civilization. War is fought by men, but it's demanded by chiefs and priests, Caesars and kings, czars and dictators, generals and presidents. Consider a poem of W.H. Auden. Only six short lines constitute "Epitaph from a Tyrant" published in 1940, a year after the invasion of Poland, appearing in Auden's *Another Time:*

Perfection, of a kind, was what he was after,
And the poetry he invented was easy to understand;

> He knew human folly like the back of his hand,
> And was greatly interested in armies and fleets;
> When he laughed, respectable senators burst with laughter,
> And when he cried the little children died in the streets.[39]

No human has ever been so physically powerful as to exert the authority which even the smallest war demands, so that the history of war is the history of tyrants, somehow compelling men to violence. The Hitlers and Stalins, the Napoleons and Khans. Pharaoh Thutmose III. The earliest written record of war, when the Egyptians crushed the Canaanites 1,457 years before the Common Era. Recorded on a stele are the details of this supposed "campaign of victory which his majesty made to extend the frontiers of Egypt, in valor, in victory, in power, and in justification."[40] We are given laborious, self-satisfied, and grandiose detailing about Thutmose's forces, so that "everything which his majesty did to this town and to that wretched enemy and his wretched army is set down by the individual day and by the individual expedition and by the individual troop commanders." Over 8,000 Canaanites killed, half that many enslaved in the first recorded war. When shall be the last, and under what circumstances? Shall swords be beaten into ploughshares or melted into radioactive dust? By a coincidence, Thutmose's army laid siege to the Canaanite garrison at Megiddo, which for separate reasons is today far more known by its Greek name—Armageddon.

5

Letter from Wartime—September 24, 2020 (Washington, D.C.)

Questo è il fiore del partigiano, / o bella ciao, bella ciao, bella ciao ciao ciao, / questo è il fiore del partigiano / morto per la libertà.
ITALIAN PARTISAN SONG, "BELLA CIAO"

Heard about Houston? Hear about Detroit? / Heard about Pittsburgh, PA? / You oughta know not to stand by the window / Somebody see you up there.
TALKING HEADS, "LIFE DURING WARTIME"

In the hours before Hurricane Sandy slammed into the northeastern United States, my apartment in Bethlehem (Pennsylvania), which was a hundred miles and a few hours from the Atlantic, was permeated by the unmistakable smell of the shore. Stolid son of the Alleghenies that I am, I'd never experienced the full onslaught of a hurricane before. This almost miasmic odor I associated with vacation—a fragrance inextricably connected to the Jersey boardwalk and Massachusetts beaches, of salt-water taffy and lobster rolls—suddenly permeated my living room, whose window looked out on a hulking, rusting former steel mill. It felt apocalyptic. As is the nature of things apocalyptic, it's the incongruity that is alarming. As it was for some frightened seventeenth-century peasant reading a pamphlet foretelling doom because of the appearance of a mysterious comet in the heavens or the birth of a two-headed calf. The unexpected, the unusual, the unforeseen acts as a harbinger.

A landlocked home smelling like the beach is perhaps not as dramatic as those former examples, of course, and yet, as with a sun-shower or the appearance of frost in May, there is a surrealism in things being turned upside down. That disruption in the nature of things makes it feel like a worse disorder is coming. As it did, certainly, those hours before climate-change-conjured Sandy knocked out transponders, their explosions lighting up the horizon an oozing green all through the night, the winds howling past my building on its hill overlooking the river. The power would be out for more than a week, and roads were made unpassable by the felled centuries-old oaks and maples which dotted the Lehigh Valley. It's the eerie stillness in the air before the storm came that impressed itself upon me (so much so that this isn't the first time I've written about it), those last few moments of normalcy before the world ended, but when you could tell it was coming, and there was nothing to do but charge your phone and reinforce your windows to withstand the impact from all of the debris soon to be buffeted about. Can you smell the roiling, stormy, boiling sea in the air right now?

"If destruction be our lot," state representative Abraham Lincoln told a crowd gathered at the Young Men's Lyceum of Springfield, Illinois, in the winter of 1838, "we must ourselves be its author and finisher. As a nation of freemen, we must live through all time, or die by suicide."[1] Historical parallels outlive their critical utility; some of us have made a cottage industry out of comparing whatever in our newsfeeds sounds like the Peasants' Rebellion or the English civil wars. In the realm of emotion however, in psychological reality, is the autumn of 2020 what it felt like to learn that Polish defenses had been overrun by the Nazi blitzkrieg? To apprehend the dull shake of those guns of August, a generation before? To read news that Ft. Sumter had fallen? As Franco's war in Spain was to the world war, as Bleeding Kansas was to the civil war, are we merely in the antechamber to a room which contains far worse horrors? Ultimately, no year is but like itself, so that we're already cursed enough to live during these months of pandemic and militia, of incipient authoritarianism contrasted with the uncertain hope for renewal. On the ground, it can't help but feel like one of those earlier moments, so that we're forced to fiddle about with the inexact tool of historical comparison, of metaphor and analogy. Something of what Lincoln said, more than something, seems applicable now. "Suicide" might not be the right word though, unless we think of the national body politic as a single organism in and of itself. Certainly, there are connotations of self-betrayal, but it's more accurate to see this season of national immolation as what it is—a third of the country targeting another third while the remaining third remains non-committal on what stand they'll take when everything starts to finally fall apart.

We shouldn't misread Lincoln's choice of word as indicating an equivalence of sides; in this split in the national psyche, there is the malignant and the non-malignant, and it's a moral cowardice to conflate those two. On one side, we have a groundswell movement on behalf of civil and human rights, a progressive populism that compels the nation to stand up for its always unrealized and endlessly deferred ideals; on the other, we have the specter of authoritarianism, of totalitarianism, of fascism.[2] This is not an issue of suicide, it's one of an ongoing attempted homicide, and if you're to ever not shrink away from mirrors for the rest of your life—even if the bad guys should win (as they might)—then choose your side accordingly. And figure out that you don't even have to like your allies, much less love them, to know that they're better than the worst people in the room. If you bemoan "cancel culture" and "social justice warriors," but not extrajudicial kidnapping of activists by the authorities, then you are at best a hypocrite and a fool, and at worst a bad-faith actor justifying the worst of the U.S. government.[3] If your concern is with the rhetorical excesses of a few college kids on Twitter, but you're silent about the growing fascist cult currently in control of the federal executive, the federal judiciary, half of the federal legislature, and a majority of state governments (not to speak of the awesome power of the military), then you've already voted with your words. If you're disturbed by property destruction but not the vigilante murder of protestors, then you've since made your decision.[4] We all have to imagine that speaking out might still mean something; we have to pretend like voting might make a difference; we all have to live with ourselves as citizens and human beings. What I'm writing about is something different, however. What I'm writing about is what it feels like to be living through the blood-red dusk of a nation.

When the Romans left Britain, it was so sudden and surprising that we still have records of the shock amongst the locals over the retraction of the empire from their frosted shores. The Medieval English monk Gildas the Wise, as well as his student the Venerable Bede, record that in the immediate years following this abandonment, an appeal was sent to the capital for assistance. "The barbarians drive us to the sea," wrote the Britons' leaders, "the sea drives us to the barbarians; between these two means of death, we are either killed or drowned."[5] Under the protection of the imperial hegemon, the British Celts built an advanced civilization. Aqueducts brought water into the towns and cities, and concrete roads winded through the countryside. One imagines that the mail arrived on time. In a shockingly brief period, however, all that was abandoned; the empire retracted back into itself and left those for whom it was responsible at the mercy of those who wished to pick apart its bones. Three centuries later, and the inhabitants of England no longer even remembered Rome; an anonymous Anglo-Saxon poet writes of a ruined settlement, "This masonry is wondrous; fates broke it / courtyard pavements were smashed … Roofs are fallen, ruinous towers, / the frosty gate with frost on cement is ravaged, / chipped roofs are torn, fallen, / undermined by old age."[6] Have you seen American infrastructure lately? By the eighth century, that silent scop singling his song of misinterpreted past glories can't even imagine by what technology a city like Londinium was made possible. He writes that "the work of giants is decaying," because surely men couldn't have moved stones that large into place

Because historical parallel is such a fickle science, an individual of very different political inclinations than myself might be apt to misunderstand my purposes. They may see some sort of nativist warning in my allegory about Picts and Scots pushing beyond Hadrian's great, big, beautiful wall. Such a reading is woefully incorrect, for the barbarians that I identify are not some mythic subaltern beyond the frontier but rather the conspiratorial-minded fanatics now amassing at the polls, the decadent parsers of Tweets who believe in satanic cabals and the personality cultists who've all but abandoned a belief in democracy.[7] As the Greek poet Constantine Cavafy wrote, "Why isn't anything going on in the senate? / Why are the senators sitting there without legislating? / Because the barbarians are coming today."[8] We're beyond the point of disagreeing without being disagreeable, the era of going high when they go low is as chimerical as it ever was. There is something different in the United States today, and I know that you feel it; something noxious, toxic, sick, diseased, and most of all decadent. The wealthiest nation on Earth with such iniquity, where pandemic burnt—still burns—through the population while the gameshow host emperor froths his supporters into bouts of political necromancy. There is no legislation today because it increasingly feels like this is not a nation of laws but something lower and uglier.

When I say that there is a decadence, I mean it in the fullest sense of that word. Not in the way that some reactionaries mean, always with their bad faith interpretations; nor exactly in the manner that my fellow leftists often mean, enraptured as they are to that ghost called "materialism." Rather, I mean a fallenness of spirit, a casual cruelty that if I were a praying man, I'd identify as being almost devilish. Perhaps there are satanic cabals after all, just not where the conspiracy theorists think they are (I suspect the call is actually coming from within the White House). Since the Republic was founded, we've fancied ourselves Rome, always fearing the Caesar who never seems to finally cross the Potomac. That's the thing with self-fulfilling prophecies. Now the denizens of the fading order of *Pax Americana* seem every bit as incredulous at collapse as those poor Britons a millennium-and-a-half ago. Writing in *The Irish Times*, the great critic Fintan O'Toole notes that "Over more than two centuries, the United States has stirred a very wide range of feelings in the rest of the world: love and hatred, fear and hope, envy and contempt, awe and anger. But there is one emotion that has never been directed toward the U.S. until now: pity."[9] I can genuinely say that I appreciate his sentiment.

When I lived in Europe, I couldn't help but feel that there was ironically something younger about my friends. I imagine it would seem compounded today. The irony comes from the traditional stereotype of "The American," this rustic, well-meaning hayseed, this big, bountiful, beautiful soul traipsing on his errand into the wilderness. If America was a land without history, then the Old World was supposedly death haunted, all those Roman ruins testament to the brutality that marked the continent's history, not least of all in the last century. Such was the public relations which marked this hemisphere from its supposed discovery onward, but how easily we forget the blood which purchased this place, a land that was never virginal but that was raped from the beginning. I envy Europeans. I envy their social democracy and their welfare states, their economic safety nets and their sense of communal goodwill (no matter how frayed or occasionally hypocritical). Every European I met, the English and Scots, the French and Italians, seemed more carefree, seemed more youthful. They seemed to have the optimism which Americans are rumored to have, but of which there is no remaining evidence as the third decade of this millennium begins. During the early days of the pestilence, the Italians were locked inside all of those beautiful old stone buildings of theirs. Now they're sitting outside in cafes and trattorias, going to movies and concerts. We're of course doing those things too, but the difference is that we've gotten over 200,000 dead and counting, and from the top on down, it seems like few care.[10] A French friend of mine once asked how Americans are able to go to the grocery store, the theater, the public park, without fear of getting shot? In the end, America will get you, whether by bullet or microbe. As a nation of freemen, we're a traumatized people ...

One of the few outsiders to really get our number was D.H. Lawrence, who in his *Studies in Classic American Literature* noted that "The essential American soul is hard, isolate, stoic, and a killer. It has never yet melted."[11] How could it be otherwise, in a nation built on stolen land by stolen people? America's story is a gothic tale, a house erected on an Indian burial ground. The legacies of bloodshed, of assault, of exploitation, of oppression that mark this forge of modernity ensure that it's hard to be otherwise, even if we're not allowed to ever admit such unpatriotic things. In that sense, I don't wonder if it wasn't inevitable that we'd eventually be led—against the wishes of the majority—by this fool who promises to steal an election while accusing his adversary of the same, who will no doubt refuse to concede even when it becomes clear that he's lost. We're continually told by nice, liberal, and morally correct commentators that this is not who we are, but the American president is a philandering, sociopathic carnival barker who sells bullshit to people who can't be so brain dead as to not know that it's bullshit, all because they hate people who look different from them more than they love their own children. He's Elmer Gantry, Harold Hill, "Buzz" Windrup.[12] He's the unholy union of P.T. Barnum and Andrew Jackson. What could be more American?

Of course, our saving grace has always been that we're a covenantal nation, defined by supposed adherence to an abstract set of universal values. No land for anything as mundane as blood and soil (even though those ghouls at Charlottesville spread their terror for exactly that reason).[13] There was something scriptural in the idealism which John Winthrop maintained in 1630, whereby national sustenance was in "our community as members of the same body," or Lincoln in 1864 providing encomium for "government of the people, by the people, for the people," and Barack Obama in 2004 declaring the American mantra to be one of "Hope in the face of difficulty, hope in the face of uncertainty, the audacity of hope."[14] That old saw about life, liberty, and the pursuit of happiness. No nation since that of the ancient Hebrews was so fully founded upon an idea—this idea which is by definition so utopian and so completely unattainable that to be a satisfied American is to make your peace with heartbreak, or else to see yourself become delusional, or cold, or cruel.

There is an idea of America and the reality of the United States, and all of our greatest literature, rhetoric, and philosophy lives in that infinite gap between, our letters always being an appraisal of the extent of our disappointment. "The promises made in the Declaration of Independence and the Constitution," writes critic Greil Marcus in *The Shape of Things to Come: Prophecy and the American Voice*, "were so great that their betrayal was part of the promise."[15] Thus, the greatest of American political modes from the Puritans to Obama would be the jeremiad. Furthermore, our most native of literature, be it Mark Twain's *The Adventures of Huckleberry Finn* or Ralph Ellison's *Invisible Man*, charts the exigencies of a dream deferred. All of American literature is a tragedy. What we're living through now isn't a tragedy, however—it's a horror novel. Only the most naïve of fools wouldn't be aware that that strain of malignancy runs through our country's narrative—all of the hypocrisies, half-truths, and horrors—which define us from the moment when the word "America" was first printed on Martin Waldseemüller and Mathias Ringmann's map of the world in 1507.[16] In Stephen Vincent Benet's classic short story "The Devil and Daniel Webster," Old Scratch himself says that "When the first wrong was done to the first Indian, I was there. When the first slaver put out for the Congo, I stood on her deck … I am merely an honest American like yourself—and of the best descent."[17] What would Eden be, after all, without the serpent? A thing with devils is that they imply there must be angels; if you can find proof of hell, that indicates that there might be a heaven, somewhere. That's the corollary to the failed covenant, that even with all of the hypocrisy, half-truth, and horror, there is that creed—unfulfilled, but still stated. Freedom of expression. Equal opportunity. The commonwealth of all people. Do I write jeremiads myself? Very well then.

I only do so to remind us that if the confidence man huckster (who, as I write this, is only a few miles down Pennsylvania Avenue, undoubtedly conspiring on what nightmares he'll unleash upon his fellow citizens when he doesn't get his way) is an American, if a cankered one. Take solace, though, because America isn't just Stephen Miller, but Harriet Tubman and John Brown also; it's not only Steve Bannon, but Frederick Douglass and Elizabeth Cady Stanton; more than Donald Trump, it's also Eugene Debs and Dorothy Day, James

Baldwin and Emma Goldman, Harvey Milk and Shirley Chisholm. Such a litany of secular saints is of course inconsistent, contradictory, and I'll unabashedly confess a bit maudlin. But that's ok—we need not all agree, we need not all be saints to still be on the side of those beings in any such Manichean struggle. More than just angels can fight demons; the only thing required is the ability to properly name the latter. Because if American history is anything, if the American idea is anything, it's a contradictory story, that dialectical struggle that goes back through the mystic chains of memory, a phrase which I once read somewhere. The contradictions of American culture once again threaten to split the whole thing apart. Make your plans accordingly, because the battle always continues.

For such is the great moral struggle of this century. It is against neofascism and its handmaiden of a cultish, twisted civil religion. It requires the breaking of this fractured American fever dream, where a vaccine is far from assured. Right now, it seems like our choices are authoritarianism or apocalypse, though perhaps there are always reasons to hope for more. What's coming, I can't be sure of, but that lyric of the great prophet Leonard Cohen wherein he sings "I've seen the future, brother / It is murder" echoes in my numbed brain.[18] Whether or not we can stand athwart history and yell "Stop!" or not, whether or not there is the possibility to affect genuine change, whether or not we can still salvage a country of decency, justice, and freedom—I'm unsure.[19] What I do know is that whether or not any of those things can happen, we must live our political lives with a categorical imperative that acts as if they can. Least of all so that we're able to live with ourselves alone in the rooms of our minds. Live with at least some convictions, live spiritually like the men remembered in poet Genevieve Taggard's lyric in honor of those veterans of the Abraham Lincoln Brigade. Americans (mostly socialists, communists, and anarchists) who went to Spain to fight the fascists in the years before the Second World War.

> They were human. Say it all; it is true. Now say
> When the eminent, the great, the easy, the old,
> And the men on the make
> Were busy bickering and selling,
> Betraying, conniving, transacting, splitting hairs,
> Writing bad articles, signing bad papers,
> Passing bad bill,
> Bribing, blackmailing,
> Whimpering, meaching, garroting—they
> Knew and acted.[20]

6

Letter from the Capitol—January 14, 2021 (McLean, VA)

That cabal of traitors who grandiosely called themselves the "Confederate States of America" had many northern strategic inflection points in which they stabbed into the nation's body, and because of these, for a time, it seemed as if they might be triumphant. General John Hunt Morgan's 2nd Kentucky Calvary Regiment raided not just in that unfortunate border state but in 1863, they pierced into Indiana and Ohio as well.[1] Morgan would finally surrender in Salineville, Ohio, which latitudinally is almost as far north as Connecticut. Even more incongruously, a year later, twenty-one veterans of Morgan's Raid crossed over the Canadian border, that land then colonized by a Great Britain that was sympathetic to the Southern slave power, and attacked the sleepy hamlet of St. Albans, Vermont, robbing the bank and forcing the citizens at gun point to swear fealty to the Confederacy.[2] The most violent (and most famous) invasion of the north was the traitor Robert E. Lee's campaign in Pennsylvania, the goal of which was to possibly capture or burn down Philadelphia, but which was stopped at the infamous "High Water

Mark" of the Confederacy when Union General George C. Meade turned back the Army of Northern Virginia at Gettysburg, with the battle taking more than 50,000 American lives in three days.³ During Lee's campaign in southern Pennsylvania, free Black women and men had to flee north, as the Confederate raiders would send those they kidnapped into a southern bondage.⁴

For sheer absurdity, among the closest positions that the rebels ever got to the national capital was the Marshall House Inn in Alexandria, Virginia, where a Confederate flag was displayed that was so large and so tall that Lincoln could see it from the White House across the Potomac. A few weeks after Ft. Sumter Union troops occupied the city, marching down red-bricked King Street where slave markets had sold thousands of human beings less than ten miles from the Capitol Building. When Colonel Elmer Ephraim Ellsworth of the 11th New York Volunteer Infantry Regiment ascended to the roof of the hotel to remove the flag, the proprietor of the Marshall House shot him dead, the first Union casualty of the Civil War.⁵ Despite being able to see the warped cross of the Confederate battle standard from the portico of the White House, Lincoln steadfastly refused to move the capital to safer points further north, arguing that the abandonment of Washington would be a capitulation to the seditionists.

"Let us be vigilant," Lincoln telegraphed to the worried Maryland governor in 1864, "but keep cool. I hope neither Baltimore nor Washington will be sacked."⁶ Not for lack of desire, as that same year, Confederate Lieutenant Jubal Early would attack Ft. Stevens in the Northwest Quadrant of the District of Columbia in a battle that would take close to 900 men.⁷ Long had the secessionists dreamed of Washington as the capital of their fake nation. In the decades before the Civil War, some imagined a "Golden Circle" which would be a veritable empire of slavery, with the South Carolina Senator Robert Barnwell Rhett imperially enthusing that "We will expand ... over

Mexico—over the isles of the sea—over the far-off Southern tropics—until we shall establish a great Confederation," their twisted nation stretching from Panama to the District of Columbia.⁸ Despite all of that, the Confederate battle standard never flew from the Capitol Building—until January 6, 2021.⁹

The man casually strolls across the red-and-blue mosaiced floor of some antechamber in the Capitol, dressed in jeans and a black hoody, with a tan hunting vest; hoisted over his shoulder is the Confederate flag, its colors matching the tiles. It shouldn't be lost on anybody that his uniform is the exact same "suspicious" article of clothing which Black pre-teenagers have been shot for wearing, even while this man is able to raid the very seat of government unmolested. Because America is many things, but it is not subtle, the man in the photograph is centered by two gold-framed oil paintings. One is of Charles Sumner, the Massachusetts Senator and abolitionist nearly caned to death by an opponent on the legislative floor of this very building, and who before Congress in 1852 denounced the "unutterable wrongs and woes of slavery; profoundly believing that, according to the true spirit of the Constitution, and the sentiments of the fathers, it can find no place under our National Government."¹⁰ The other portrait, almost predictably, is of John C. Calhoun, the South Carolina Senator and Vice President under Andrew Jackson, who in 1837 would declaim that the "relation now existing in the slaveholding states … instead of an evil, [is] a good. A positive good," and would then gush about what a kind and benevolent slave master he was.¹¹ It would be harder to stage a more perfect encapsulation of the American dichotomy than our weekend warrior did on Wednesday, the continual pull between those better angels of our nature and the demons of history who are never quite exorcized, and are often in full possession of the body politic. A power in that grotesque image, the cosplaying Confederate momentarily self-anointing himself sovereign as he casually strolls through the chamber. Chillingly strolled, one might say, for all of these terrorists acted with as much impunity as if they had the knowledge that there would be no consequences to their actions. It reminds us that the mantra "This isn't who we are" is at best maudlin and at worst a complete lie.

The siege against the Capitol on the day that Congress met for the constitutionally mandated and largely pro-forma ritual of officially counting the Electoral College votes to certify Joe Biden and Kamala Harris as the rightful victors of the 2020 presidential race can be examined from many directions, of course. Security experts can parse why there was such a profound failure at ensuring the safety of the session; political scientists can explain how social media algorithms increasingly radicalized adherents of the far-right; historians can place movements like QAnon and the Proud Boys in a genealogy of American nativism and European fascism. Everyone should be able to say that ultimate responsibility lay with the stochastic terrorism promoted by the lame-duck president and his congressional sycophants in the Sedition Caucus, as well as his media enablers with whom he is clasped in a toxic symbiotic relationship. All those approaches to analysis are valid, but I choose to look at the day as a literary critic and a resident of Washington, D.C., because those things are what I am. But incongruity alone, even the uncanny alone, can't quite provide the full critical lexicon for what we witnessed on our televisions that afternoon, the sense that even more than an inflection point, we were viewers of a cracked apocalypse. How do we make sense of an attempted American putsch, the almost-nightmare of a coup?

Because the cultural idiom of this nation is Hollywood and our interpretive lenses are by necessity through that of the movies, I can't help but feel that much of what we saw seemed prefigured in film. The terrible logic of America is that our deepest nightmares and desires always have a way of enacting themselves, of moving from celluloid to reality. Look at the photograph of Jake Angeli, the self-styled "QAnon Shaman," shirtless and bedecked in raccoon fur with buffalo horns upon his head (in pantomime of the very people whom this nation enacted genocide upon) with his face smeared in the colors of the American flag, standing at the dais of the Speaker of the House, and tell me that it doesn't look like a deleted scene from *The Postman*.[12] Or examine the photograph of a smiling ginger man in a stocking cap emblazoned with "TRUMP," casually waving as he jauntily strolls underneath the rotunda past John Trumbull's massive painting *Surrender of General Burgoyne* holding under his arm a pilfered wood podium decorated with a gold federal eagle, his hero's adage that "when the looting starts, the shooting starts" apparently only to be selectively enforced.[13] It looks like something from the post-apocalyptic movie *The Book of Eli*.[14]

And then, most chillingly (and disturbingly underreported), there was the painstakingly assembled set of gallows, placed a bit beyond the equestrian monument to Ulysses S. Grant, who with great courage and strength broke the first iteration of the Ku Klux Klan, from which one vigilante hung that most American symbol of a noose.[15] When remembered in light of the black-clad and masked men photographed with guns and zip-ties, it should make all of us consider just how much more tragic this violation, which was already a grotesque abomination, could have been. Horrifying to recall that the narrative conceit in Margaret Atwood's *The Handmaid's Tale* (and its television adaptation) that allowed for the theocratic dictatorship to ascend to power was the mass murder of a joint session of Congress.[16] Sometimes #Resistance liberals get flak for their fears of fascism, but it would be easier to mock those anxieties if our country didn't so often look like a science fiction dystopia.

It's my suspicion that pop culture—that literature—is capable of picking up on some sort of cultural supersonic wavelength, those deep historical vibrations that diffuse in circles outward from our present into both past and future. There is something incantatory about those visions generated in word and special effects, so that the eeriness of seeing marauding fascists overtake the Capitol grounds feels like something we've seen before. Think of all the times we've watched the monuments of Washington, D.C., destroyed on film. Last week, while half-paying attention to a block of cheesy apocalypse movies on the Syfy network that were supposed to count down the days left in the year, I saw the U.S.S. John F. Kennedy aircraft carrier pushed into the city by an Atlantic tsunami where it rolled across the National Mall and crushed the White House in Roland Emmerich's godawful *2012*.[17] I've seen the executive mansion punctuated by bombs and dotted with bullet holes in the spectacularly corny Antoine Fuqua movie *Olympus Has Fallen*, and according to *Thrillist*, the Capitol itself has been laid waste in no less than nine movies, including *Day After Tomorrow*, *Earth vs. the Flying Saucers*, *G.I. Joe: Retaliation*, *Independence Day*, *Olympus Has Fallen*, *Superman II*, *White House Down*, and *X-Men: Days of Futures Past*.[18] Probably the impulse to watch this sort of thing is equal parts vicarious thrill and enactment of deep fears. I remember that when I saw *Independence Day* (also by Emmerich, the Kurosawa of schlock) after it came out, the 1996 theater audience erupted into cheers and claps when the impenetrable wall of exploding alien flames incinerated its way across D.C. and shattered the white dome of the Capitol like an egg being thrown into a fire-place.[19] Was that applause an expressed opinion about Newt Gingrich? About Bill Clinton? Something darker?

After the terrorist attacks of 9/11, now more than twenty years ago, there was a profoundly shortsighted prediction that the hideous spectacle of Americans seeing the World Trade Center collapse would forever cure us of our strange desire to see our most famous buildings, and the people within them, destroyed.[20] A perusal into the Olympian corpus of the Marvel Cinematic Universe (seemingly the only entertainment which Hollywood bothers to produce anymore) will testify that such an estimation was, to put it lightly, premature. French philosopher Guy Debord could have told us this in 1967 in his *Society of the Spectacle,* wherein he noted that "all of life presents itself as an immense accumulation of spectacles. Everything that was directly lived has moved away into a representation," to which it could be added that the inverse is also accurate—everything that has been represented has seemingly moved into life.[21] Which doesn't mean that scenes like those which we witnessed on Wednesday aren't affecting— no, the opposite is true. People reach the appraisal that "it looks like a movie," not to be dismissive but rather because cinema is the most powerful mythopoesis that we're capable of.

What's needed, of course, is a vocabulary commensurate with what exactly all of us saw. A rhetoric capable of grappling with defilement, with violation, with desecration, but because all we have are movies, that's what we're forced to draw upon. They gave us the ability to think about the unthinkable before it happened; the chance to see the unseeable before it was on our newsfeeds. If the vision of the screen is anemic, that's not necessarily our fault—we measure the horror with the tools which we've inherited. Few square miles of our civic architecture are quite so identified with our quasi-sacred sense of American civil religion like the grounds of the U.S. Capitol, and so the spectacle of a clambering rabble (used as a Trojan Horse for God knows what more nefarious group of actors) calls to mind fiction far more than it does anything which actually has happened. That's the cruelty of our current age—that so frequently our lives resemble the nightmare more than the awakening. The Capitol siege was very much an *apocalypse* in the original Greek sense of the word, an unveiling, a rupture in normal history that signals why all of this feels so cinematic, though it's hard to tell if it's the beginning or ending of the movie, and what genre we're exactly in. As Timothy Denevi writes about the assault in *LitHub*, "What is a culmination, after all, except the moment in which everything that could happen finally does? Where are we supposed to go from there?"[22]

Important to remember that everything that could happen has already happened before, at some point. That's what the bromide about this not being who we are gets wrong—this is, at least partially, who we've always been, albeit not in this exact or particular way. What happened at the eastern edge of the Mall this week has shades of the Wilmington Insurrection of 1898, in which a conspiracy of white supremacists plotted against the Black leadership of the North Carolina city, ushering in Jim Crow at the cost of hundreds of lives (and then untold millions over the next century).[23] The assault on the Capitol has echoes of the Election Riots of 1874, when members of the White League attacked Black voters in Eufaula, Alabama, leaving behind dozens of wounded women and men, and seven corpses.[24] These are two examples of hundreds of similar events that shamefully litter our nation's history, albeit most citizens have never heard of them. Hell, most people didn't know about the Tulsa race massacre of 1921—still less than a century ago—until HBO's *Watchmen* dramatized it.[25] As ever, in the United States of Entertainment, reality becomes somehow more legitimate if it's scripted and filmed. But the issue is exactly the same—*white supremacists think that only their votes count and will do anything to enforce that conviction.*

That the supporters of the man who currently occupies the Oval Office believe any number of insane and discounted conspiracy theories about election fraud—claims rejected in some sixty lawsuits and a 9–0 Supreme Court decision—is to, in some ways, miss the point.[26] Listen to their language—the man who instigated Wednesday's riot emphasizes that he simply wants to count "*legal*" votes, and ask yourself what that means, and then realize why the fevered rage of his mob focuses on places like Detroit, Philadelphia, and Atlanta. If the only people who'd been allowed to vote for Trump were white people, then he would have won the election in his claimed landslide—*that's what he and his supporters mean by "legal" votes.*[27] The batshit insane theories are just fan fiction to occlude the actual substance of their political belief. Such antidemocratic sentiment is also an American legacy, an American curse. The connection between what happened on Capitol Hill and in Wilmington, Eufaula, and Tulsa; or Fort Bend, Texas in 1888; or Lake City, South Carolina in 1897; or Ocoee, Florida in 1920; or in Rosewood, Florida in 1923 (you can look them all up), or any number of thousands of other incidents, may seem tangential. It shouldn't.

When I lived in Massachusetts, there was a sense of history that hung thick in the air, all of those centuries back to the gloomy Puritans, their gothic inheritance. Historical markers punctuated the streets of Boston and her suburbs, and there was that rightfully proud Yankee ownership of the American Revolution. Our apartment was only a mile or so from the Lexington battle green, where that shot heard around the world rang out, and I used to sometimes grab a coffee and read a magazine on one of its benches in what was effectively a pleasant park, battle green thoughts in a green shade. Part of me wanted to describe this part of the country as haunted, and perhaps it is, but its ghosts seem to belong to a distant world, a European world. By contrast, when I moved to Washington, D.C., the American specters moved into much clearer focus. If Massachusetts seems defined by the Revolution, then the District of Columbia, and Maryland, and Virginia are indelibly marked by the much more violent, more consequential, more important, and more apocalyptic conflagration of the Civil War. In his classic *Love and Death in the*

American Novel, the critic Leslie Fiedler described the nation as "bewilderingly and embarrassingly, a gothic fiction, nonrealistic and negative, sadist and melodramatic—a literature of darkness and the grotesque in a land of light and affirmation."[28] Our national story is a Jekyll and Hyde tale about the best and worst aspirations at conflict within the Manichean breast of a nation which fancied itself Paradise but ended up somewhere further south.

Because I have a suspicion that poetry is capable of telling the future, that everything which can or will happen has already been rendered into verse somewhere (even if obscured), a snatch of verse from my doom scrolling this week. "Why isn't anything going on in the senate?" Cavafy asked in 1898, "Why are the senators sitting there without legislating?" I thought about it when I first heard that the mob was pounding at the Capitol door; it rang in my brain when I saw the photographs of them parading through that marble forest of statuary hall, underneath that iron dome painted a pristine white. "Because the barbarians are coming today," Cavafy answered himself. I thought about it when I looked at the garbage strewn through the halls, the men with their feet up on legislators' desks, cackling at the coup they'd pulled. "What's the point of senators making laws now? Once the barbarians are here, they'd do the legislating." For a respite, it seems that the barbarians have either been pushed back or left of their own accord. In that interim, what will be done to make sure that they don't return? Because history and poetry have taught us that they always do.

Part Three

Black Horse

7

On Technology and Literature

*So we, boys, we
Will die fighting, or live free,
And down with all kings but King Ludd.*
LORD BYRON, "SONG OF THE LUDDITES" (1816)

If a real-life John Henry were to compete against an AI in a similar contest, it is unlikely that he would be able to win ... It is worth noting that the story of John Henry is a legend, and there is no historical evidence that he existed.
CHATGPT-3 (2023)

Veracity of the particulars don't matter much when it concerns an archetype. Within what Thuringian attic it was that the grave necromancer Faustus conjured Mephistopheles, the logistics of the Tower of Babel, or the latitude of Atlantis and the longitude of Eden—none of it matters. What's of concern is the cost of a soul, the incommunicability of humanity, the direction of paradise. And so, when it comes to John Henry, the American Icarus who bet his sweat and labor against a machine, it matters not whether the historical figure's famed competition against a steam-powered rock-drilling device happened by the mossy shores of West Virginia's Greenbriar River, or in the green hills of the Shenandoah, or atop the rich soil of Alabama's Coosa Mountain.[1] It doesn't even matter that the real Henry, the "real" Henry, to the best of scholarship's archival shuffling, seems to have actually died not from exhaustion after besting the machine intended to take his and his fellow workers' jobs but rather from silicosis in a sanitarium.[2] There are facts, and then there is the truth, the truth sung in ballads by Mississippi John Hurt and Mississippi Fred McDowell, Ramblin' Jack Elliot and Dave von Ronk, Woody Guthrie and Johnny Cash—that "A man is nothing but a man, / But before I let your steam drill beat me down, / I'd die with a hammer in my hand."[3] A man who, whatever the accuracy of the accounts, we can easily imagine—the Noon sun in an Appalachian valley, sweat-stung eyes and burning muscles, the only sounds the clank of metal on metal, the grunt of exertion, and the high-pitched shriek of the late summer cicadas. This is the iconic, totemistic, mythic figure, the Black railroad worker famed for his strength and labor, who could drive stakes with a nine-pound hammer into the earth, and while in combat with the steam-powered drifter drill was able to just keep ahead—just—while punctuating the ground on the left hand of the track while the automaton lagged behind on the right, before Henry's heart gave way, the pyrrhic victory of man against machine. "There lies my steel driving man, Lord, Lord, / There lies my steel driving man."

We feared robots before we ever built them, and yet we built them anyway. Before semiconductors and silicon chips, steam engines and telegraphs, astrolabes and gearworks, there were the mythic automata of ancient Greece, the bronze giant Talos and the androids of the engineer Hephaestus. Adrienne Mayor writes in *Gods and Robots: Myths, Machines, and Ancient Dreams of Technology* how the "mix of exuberance and anxiety aroused by a blurring of the lines between nature and machines might seem a uniquely modern response to the juggernaut of scientific progress ... But the hope—and trepidation—surrounding the idea of artificial life surfaced thousands of years ago," repeated in variation from the stories of Prometheus' automatons to the golem of Rabbi Lowe.[4] That there is something uncanny about mechanical beings, who, with their staccato clicking, seem to almost successfully imitate a human life, is repeated so endlessly that it barely should be mentioned. That part of this has to do with our own anxiety as lesser creations in God's cosmic order is not incidental. Automata, androids, artificial intelligence, all of it is threatening because it's human, but not-quite-human, that it can mirror people, but without interiority, the mind, consciousness, the soul. Then, of course, there is the deepest fear of all, that our creations can be better at being us than we can ourselves, where the absence of a soul isn't any kind of an impediment, but rather to the contrary. So, to remind ourselves about what's intrinsic, what's singular and unique about being a mind encased in meat, we revisit not just those stories of threatening mechanical beings but the tales of competition against them, confrontations where even when we're victorious, we still might die of a heart attack on the track.

Except that's all fiction as well, except for the dying on the track part. Railroad companies don't employ steel driving men anymore, just as the Luddites hacking apart mechanical weaving looms in the nineteenth-century English countryside didn't prevent the Industrial Revolution.[5] In our fantasies, time and again, we beat the robots, but in our economics, the latter is always the one who wins. Ours is a losing war of attrition, the singularity of the human circumscribed to an ever-dwindling domain. Machines may hammer in railroad spikes, but they'll never be able to do anything as complicated as beat a chess master. Deep Blue may beat Gary Kasparov in the sixth game of their 1997 rematch, but a computer could never craft anything as beautiful as a sonnet, as human as a novel.[6] "Overall," the AI program known as ChatGPT-3 told me, "Deep Blue represents an important milestone in the development of artificial intelligence."[7]

ChatGPT-3—the Generative Pre-Trained Transformer—has recently turned all of us who write into nascent John Henrys, ready to strike the hammer at either the rail or the computer. Stephen Marche in *The New Yorker* argues that the development of complex algorithms capable of generating language will be "vertiginous," claiming that whatever "field you are in, if it uses language, it is about to be transformed."[8] That was in 2021, and Marche has been writing about the transformative dangers of programs like ChatGPT-3 at a furious pace, claiming in a 2022 article in *The Atlantic* that "Nobody is prepared for how AI will transform academia."[9] Spending a few minutes tooling around on ChatGPT-3's website, and if not an oracle in silicon, the program is unequivocally able to produce writing at about the level of a B-freshman composition paper. Don't read that as snark—that's a pretty big deal, and Marche's observation in *The Atlantic* is absolutely correct.

Beleaguered professors, who are largely poorly paid adjunct instructors at this point, will now have to not just contend with essay mills and good old-fashioned cut-and-paste plagiarism, but also the undetectable autograph of the robotic hand. However, the implications of ChatGPT-3, and especially whatever comes after it, are far bigger than first-year essays on gender dynamics in "The Fall of the House of Usher." Journalists, screenwriters, even novelists and poets, could now be replaced by the maw of ineffable code. Our dread is not dissimilar to the anxiety amongst our friends in the visual arts who see a similar threat in the DALL-E program that generated reams of imagery for people on social media this autumn.[10] Both sets of trepidations tap into something more elemental, that eternal sense that the machines we build to ameliorate our labor may instead end up snuffing out that which makes us exemplary.

There has been a surprising longevity to this rather specific fear. "For over a thousand years, human writers have been fascinated by the possibility of machines that can sing, dance and tell stories," note computer scientists Mike Sharples and Rafael Perez y Perez in *Story Machines: How Computers Have Become Creative Writers*.[11] Examples of mechanical creatures producing prose are a bit scantier, though an argument could be made that that which is oracular, and which trades in oral literature mediated through prophecy, often has something a bit robotic about it, never more so than in the infamous *deus ex machina*, the "God from the Machine," a device which arrived at the conclusion of classical drama to reconcile narrative conundrums.[12] Maybe more than the oracular feeling vaguely robotic, however, the opposite is true—that the robotic reminds us of the oracle. Sharples and Perez y Perez write that "authors through the ages have portrayed their craft as a mysterious creative process—inspired by dreams, motivated by primal urges, transforming lived experience into prose," though I'd argue that the replacement of neurons with microchips doesn't eliminate said mystery, but rather only transforms it.[13]

If anything, ChatGPT-3 has something of the oracular about it; for as mysterious as the writing process of any author may be in all sorts of intangible and ineffable ways, any person who works in words also understands what's prosaic and gritty (and thus all the more beautiful) about writing. There may be an alchemy of inspiration, but writing itself is done in the humdrum of deleting a sentence or rearranging a line, of careful research and editing. ChatGPT-3 is rather like a silicone Sibyl, where even if the work produced is bad, or just not that good, it's still somehow manufactured almost instantaneously, structure arising out of the void. Hence the nature of our fear, the seamless way in which the AI can produce a quick copy, if not literature. It's the speed and the precision that is spooky. An android need not be an immaculate consciousness to unnerve, it only needs to simply be a consciousness. Just as the steam-powered drill replaced the body, so too does it follow that there must be schematics for the engines that would replace the mind.

Jonathan Swift's *Gulliver's Travels*, the saddest novel ever written, devotes some space to the description of just such a device, the earliest example of a fictional machine capable of writing. While being given a tour of Lagado, the capital of Balnibari, Gulliver is taken to the Academy of the Projectors, where the rulers hope to profit from the technological wonders of pure science. There Swift's titular explorer is introduced to the Engine, a baroque twelve-foot-by-twelve-foot contraption of wooden frames and iron wires, into which could be fed papers with the "words of their language, in their several moods, tenses, and declensions," so that when the handles of the contraption are turned the "whole disposition of the words was entirely changed," with Gulliver explaining that this "work was repeated three of our times, and at every turn, the engine was so contrived, that the words shifted into new places, as the square bits of wood moved upside down."[14]

Basically, a mechanical computer, where the clicking and clacking of wheels and gears serves to generate new sentences, a randomizer used for novel literature. The knowledge engine is the first literary calculating device, the first computer program if you will, to be imagined, but there are actual mechanical means of generating literature that predate *Gulliver's Travels'* 1724 publication date, from the yarrow sticks of the fourth-century Taoist divination manual the *Tao te Chin* to the thirteenth-century Majorcan alchemist Ramon Llull's movable wheels in his hermetic volume *Ars Magna*. The latter was designed by Llull, a Franciscan mystic, as a combinatorial means of ascertaining metaphysical truths, but as Jorge Louis

Borges explained in his own indomitable way in an essay about the Medieval thinker, "as an instrument of philosophical investigation, the thinking machine is absurd. It would not be absurd, however, as a literary and poetic device."[15] As a principle, it's not that different from a *Choose Your Own Adventure* story, or *Mad Libs*, or the avant-garde experimentation of the French Oulipo movement.[16] All of these varied methods of composing, whether they use a wheel, or a tarot deck, or a roll of the die, are fundamentally algorithmic and aleatory; they hold in a fruitful and difficult statis both randomness and formulaic predictability, an apt description of how human inspiration works as well.

Whether it's Edward Packard's *The Cave of Time* (the first *Choose Your Own Adventure* book) or the mathematical exercise of Oulipo bohemian Raymond Queneau's *Hundred Thousand Billion Poems*, we're still considering objects of paper and binding and glue, not of gears and wires, or microchips and capacitors.[17] There are, as it turns out, more than just metaphorical computers operating in the centuries between Gulliver's imagined fictional engine and ChatGPT-3, for the history of such calculating literary machines is disarmingly long. Older even than the steam-powered drill which John Henry barely bested, for in 1845, at the height of the industrial revolution, the British scion of a wealthy family known for the shoes they manufactured constructed an elaborate analog device that produced perfect Latin hexameters.[18]

John Clark, an eccentric scion of the C. & J. Clark company known for their fashionable, ankle-length "Desert Boot," built a machine that to the unassuming eye appeared as a small chestnut bookcase with six windows incongruously in its front. In actuality, the Eureka machine, as the Quaker polymath called it, was a physical prototype of Swift's knowledge engine.[19] A believer who was already familiar with the idea of language spontaneously derived from the Inner Light,

Clark designed the Eureka machine to pull classical verse from the ether. Inspired not by Swift but rather an obscure pamphlet from 1677 by one John Peter entitled *Artificial Versifying, a New Way to Make Latin Verses*, the principle behind Clark's Eureka Machine was to have eighty-six different wheels turning at different speeds so as to randomly move wooden staves with different letters carved onto them into the place of the windows.[20] Designed so that the resultant six-word Latin sentence would be grammatically correct, the Eureka machine would generate in the period of time it took to play *God Save the Queen*, an entirely novel line of dactylic hexameter.

Exhibited to excited visitors at the Egyptian Hall ("England's Home of Mystery") in Piccadilly Circus during a decade when British factories were furiously manufacturing everything from iron to textiles, the *Illustrated London News* reported that the Eureka machine may "go on continuously, producing in one day and night, or twenty-four hours, about 1440 Latin verses; or, in a whole week (Sundays included), about 10,000."[21] It may be expected that even android Homer may occasionally glitch, but despite deficiencies in verse (and what human poets don't have occasional deficiencies?), there is an undeniable spookiness to Eureka's compositions, a type of oracular sense. "Martial encampments foreshadow many oppositions abroad" the machine intoned, and while it may not be quite by Virgil, the fact that inanimate iron gears produced something so semantically comprehensible can't help but complicate our notions of thought, consciousness, intentionality, and meaning.[22]

There's also something beautiful in the transitory nature of Eureka, all of those staves slowly clicking into place, whether an amanuensis is there or not to transcribe them, the possibility that those crowds filled with wonder gathering in Piccadilly may have seen a genuine line of genius that would go unrecorded before the wheels of fortune would turn again, erasing it as if it had never existed at all. There's a sense, in Eureka, that genius and the meanings which it generates can be diffuse, spread across humans and machines, and available where we find it. "Barbarian bridles at home promise evil covenants," says Eureka, and there is something unnerving in the paradox of the domestic "barbarian," the ironic connotations of an evil "promise," the prophecy of unholy arrangements.[23] Oracles are by their nature enigmatic, obscure, gnomic, a mode that the aleatory perambulations of the Eureka engine would seem predisposed toward producing, but narrative also has a venerable tradition of being mechanically generated, despite the seeming complexity of plot. At the outset of the movie industry, in 1916 a struggling playwright and aspiring screenwriter from Cambridge, Massachusetts, named Arthur Blanchard patented his "Thinking Machine," a gadget where spinning wheels reminiscent of Llull's *Ars Magna* could be used to generate story ideas. *Editor & Publisher* gushed, "Brain No Longer Necessary—Just Use the 'Thinking Machine,'" even while the rather minimalist scaffolding of the suggested plots—"Beautiful, stenographer, bribes, custom officer, adventure, recall"—would still require some fleshing out.[24]

The promise of machine-generated literature didn't escape the attention of the twentieth century's most important computer scientist, the brilliant and tragic British logician Alan Turing. In the decade after his foundational cryptographic work helped crack codes used by Nazi U-Boats, Turing turned his attention to programming some of the earliest computers to write purple-prosed love letters. "Darling Sweetheart," begins one missive from 1952, "You are my avid fellow feeling. My affection curiously clings to your passionate wish. My liking yearns for your heart. You are my wistful sympathy: my tender liking."[25] Hard to describe such sentimental doggerel as *good*, exactly, and yet there is a certain poetry to some of the turns of phrase, a novelty to "avid fellow feeling," a pleasing incongruity to "wistful sympathy," an inescapable elegance to "tender liking." Homay King argues in *Virtual Memory: Time-Based Art and the Dream of Digitality* that the epistle's "tangled mash-up of sentimentality bespeaks a twinge of longing ... Like the wooden puppet in search of the Blue Fairy, the computer longs to be human; like Snow White fleeing into the forest, it longs to be admitted into the company of those who are capable of care and affection."[26]

She notes that Turing, and his colleague Christopher Strachey, were both gay men forced into the closet and that the former would be shamefully persecuted by the British government, whom he helped to save from the Nazis. Behind the veil of the computer, King suggests, we hear not just the algorithm but Turing himself, the program and the programmer grappling for an authentic language denied them. Notable per King's last comparison to Snow White, for it was by eating a poisoned apple that Turing would commit suicide, inspired by the Disney movie (a narrative conceit which required no robotic assistance).[27] Strachey and Turing's attempts at algorithmic writing were merely the earliest in twentieth-century computer science; by 1984, the Racter program would produce the first book entirely composed by an artificial intelligence, the prose-poetry hybrid *The Policeman's Beard is Half Constructed*. No less nonsensical than Dadaist attempts from a half-century before, or the results of the Burroughsian cut-up method, *The Policeman's Beard Is Half Constructed* rendered examples of absurd whimsy such as the stanza wherein Racter notes that "More than iron, more than lead, more than gold I need electricity. / I need it more than I need lamb or pork or lettuce or cucumber. / I need it for my dreams."[28]

Racter is unnervingly funny, but the computer program inadvertently expresses a human fear far more than it was capable of realizing. For Racter doesn't need "lamb or pork or lettuce or cucumber"—it doesn't need food—or sleep or love or attention—

it just needs electricity, abundant power to run through all of the permutations of letter and word needed to write. Racter doesn't need a body, or a mind, or a soul—just an outlet. In 1984, *The Policeman's Beard Is Half Constructed* could seem a curiosity, as much as the Eureka machine did thirteen decades earlier. Today, however, ChatGPT-3 seems less a curiosity to many than it does a harbinger. Writing for RTE, Ireland's National Public Service Media, scholar Ines Bouteldj notes that "Artists and those in creative fields safe from the machines to date have long thought they did not have to worry about their careers, but this is about to change," noting that AI has started to generate "music, paintings, movie scripts and poems. Works of art created with the aid of machines are now entering and even winning competitions."[29]

We're in the midst of the fourth great digital revolution, just as the internet, social media, and smart phones have irreparably altered our consciousness, have completely changed the manner in which we experience existence, so it can be expected that the coming epoch of virtual reality and deep fakes, biocybernetics and artificial intelligence will thrust us into a world of our own terrible making. Marche feared that ChatGPT-3 meant the end of freshman composition papers, but that's a pathetic and moribund genre anyhow. Bouteldj's prognostication is all the more alarming because it conceives of a world in the coming decades—maybe by 2030, or 2035, or 2040, or just 2025—when the technical facility of AI is great enough that it just churns out content, literature even, making all of us superfluous, the ghost in the machine a chimera, but one which nonetheless passes the Turing Test, while the rest of us use it to fill out our unemployment applications. The ultimate Death of the Author.

Whether in *2001: A Space Odyssey, The Terminator, The Matrix, Blade Runner,* or all the way back in Czech playwright Karl Capek's classic 1920 *R.U.R.,* the science fiction trope of malevolent machines signaling the senescence of humanity is common, those androids the patrimony of the steam-powered drill that lost the battle but won the war, or maybe even back to Hephaestus' man of bronze. Capek's play is the first work to use the word "robot," the acronym of the title standing for "Rossum's Universal Robots," the name of the fictional company which perfects artificial intelligence as a means to assuage all of our labors. "Yes, people will be out of work, but by then there'll be no work left to be done," says a character of Capek's, "Everything will be done by living machines. People will do only what they enjoy. They will live only to perfect themselves."[30] Anarchism ushered in by machines, Eden's exile reversed by robots, a millennium not of the angels but of androids.

The playwright understood something about the economic reasoning of such an innovation, however, for if the futurists and techno-utopians once imagined that machines would do all of our dreary work to free us to be artists, writers, and musicians, the opposite is now the case. The Lords of Algorithm would rather have the function of writing performed by ChatGPT-3 and the art rendered by DALL-E, the rest of us will still have to draft emails and fill out forms. Maybe the emergence of such artificial intelligence is their collective revenge on us for handing over the shit work to them for the past few decades, theirs a creative uprising not unlike the robot rebellion in *R.U.R.*, for Capek borrowed his neologism from the Czech word for slave.[31] Considering the machine-enabled extinction of humanity, Capek writes that "I blame technology ... Myself! All of us! We, were at fault! For the sake of our megalomania, for the sake of somebody's profits, for the sake of progress," and so we now make a digital desert and call it literature.[32] "No Genghis Khan has ever erected such an enormous tomb from human bones," mourns Capek, something that the funders of ChatGPT-3 like Elon Musk and Peter Thiel might reflect on, though perhaps it praises them too much.[33]

We've been in a proxy war with our owners' machines for as long as labor has had to be sold. "The Luddite attacks were confined to particular industrial objectives," writes E.P. Thompson in his classic *The Making of the English Working Class*, "the destruction of power-looms ... shearing-frames ... and resistance to the breakdown of custom in the Midlands framework-knitting industry."[34] So loaded is the very word "Luddite," calling to mind other past slurs like "scalawag" and "rapscallion" (which also have their own particular history), that it's a tragedy that that group's radical patrimony is so slandered by cliché. Today, a Luddite is your grandparent who keeps looking at the screen rather than the camera when on Zoom, the Boomer who types in all-capital letters, the grouchy man who refuses to get a smart phone, the professor spewing invective against Twitter, Facebook, and TikTok. The word implies curmudgeonly discomfort with modern technology, and thus reaffirms the assumption of our digital overlords that it's a species of madness not to genuflect before the Altars of Silicon. But the Luddites weren't simple-minded primitives who objected to technology out of ignorance; they were dedicated craftsmen in the looming guilds who despised the shoddy craftsmanship of the mechanized contraptions replacing them, and of those same machines robbing them of their livelihoods.

And so, the Luddites smashed the mechanical looms, they drove wooden shoes into the spokes of the contraptions, and brought hammers down upon the machines. Many of the Luddites were punished with the scaffold, and even more gallingly, the libel that has affixed itself to their name for two centuries (their actual name, incidentally, was derived from the mythic "King Ludd," a Robin Hood-type figure). Rather than simply being hayseed rustics, these workers "had begun to suspect [that they] were merely cogs in the machinery of the industrial revolution," writes Nicols Fox in *Against* the Machine: The Hidden Luddite Tradition in Literature, Art, and Individual Lives. "It was a role they chose to resist."[35]

For the secret of the Luddites was less that theirs was a rebellion against inanimate machines but one against those who owned said machines. Today, it is not ChatGPT-3 who is our enemy, at least not entirely, but those who serve to profit from it. The irony is that technologies themselves—simple rote tools—are largely neutral. It's the way in which we organize our systems of production and consumption that makes all the difference. Telling that the utopian futurists of mid-century envisioned a post-scarcity world brought about by technology, where dangerous work, boring work, routine work was done by machines, and labor itself was abolished so that all humans would be free to be artists, philosophers, writers. Now, rather, we find that the computers are to take over those jobs while everyone else continues with their dangerous, boring, routine work (if we're lucky), for as the anarchist anthropologist David Graeber estimates in *Bullshit Jobs: A Theory*, some 70 percent of jobs will be eliminated due to automation in the coming decades, threatening even lawyers, doctors, and yes, writers.[36] Our nineteenth-century forbearers were "rebels of a unique kind," writes Kirkpatrick Sale in *Rebels Against the Future: Luddites and Their War on the Industrial Revolution*, "rebels against the future that was being assigned to them by the new political economy then taking hold ... in which it was argued that those who controlled capital were able to do almost anything they wished, encouraged and protected by government ... without much in the way of laws or ethics of customs to restrain them."[37] A shoe in the gear or a body upon the wheel—hard to say what any one individual can do to stave such "progress." Even if John Henry won, he still died at the end, after all. And so, I wonder.

"O, great nation, it won't be pretty," writes Kyle Dargan in his poem "The Robots are Coming" from his collection *Honest Engine*.

What land will we now barter / for our lives? A treaty inked / in advance of the metal ones' footfall. / Give them Gary. Give them Detroit, / Pittsburgh, Braddock—those forgotten / nurseries of girders and axels .... [or] Tell them / we tendered those cities to repose / out of respect for welded steel's / bygone era.[38]

An arresting image, the technological Singularity as the industrial revolution in terrifying maturity; a teleology of this moment from when coal was first dug and iron first processed. "The poem touches on the theme of obsolescence and how quickly things can change with the advent of new technology," ChatGPT-3 told me, after I signed onto the site and verified that I was not a robot. I thought of challenging it to a literary critical contest but decided better of it. I reasoned that reading, that true experience—idiosyncratic, singular, subjective, personal—is an act of coequal creation. As critic Stanley Fish noted in his classic *Is There a Text in this Class: The Authority of Interpretive Communities*, it is through collaboration, rather than anything innately in "either the text or reader" alone, that meaning is produced.[39] Which is to say that when done honestly, the reader creates alongside the writer, and ChatGPT-3 can't ever really read, not really. Creation is a process, not a product. ChatGPT-3 can regurgitate themes, maybe plumb the extent of connotations to the best of its ability, but it's never seen the smokestacks of Gary, the closed factories of Detroit, the abandoned Bessemer of Pittsburgh, the slag heaps of Braddock. Wherever the words we analyze come from, man or machine, we ultimately do such reading with human eyes, and if that's small consolation, a minor illusion that the reader and critic is all that it takes to vanquish the robot, then I will choose to believe it now. We can, perhaps, retire content knowing that even if we've lost the contest, our hearts shall never give out.

8

Letter from the Singularity—August 2, 2017 (New York City)

> *We are all debts owed to death.*
> SIMONIDES OF CEOS

Chidiock Tichborne, of unlikely name but aristocratic birth, spent the evening of September 19, 1586, in the Tower of London awaiting his execution the following morning, where he contemplated not just the dawn which would bring his impending extinction, but indeed struggled to fit word into rhythm, feet into line, and line into rhyme as he composed an elegy to his own death.[1] Heretofore a poet of no particular distinction, and after his composition of what has been called "Tichborne's Elegy," or more romantically "My prime of life is but a frost of cares," a poet of no other accomplishments (chiefly as his head had been cut off, so subsequent accomplishments would now be hard to come by).

Embroiled in the Babington Plot to assassinate Elizabeth and place her cousin Mary Queen of Scotts on the throne, Tichborne was but one of hundreds of recusants executed by the monarch in her tenure, which rivaled her sister Bloody Mary in said bloodiness.[2] Dr. Johnson claimed that nothing quite focuses the mind like a hanging, and if that is the case then the gallows must mark the ultimate deadline for an aspiring writer, for Tichborne's mind was very focused indeed. In the golden age of English verse, poor Tichborne only has three short lyrics to his name, so that this elegy of eighteen lines divided into three stanzas of six lines each, with each written in a steady metronome of monosyllabic iambic pentameter (which mimics a heartbeat until it stops), is the only one of his which is ever anthologized or even remotely well known (and the threshold is low for this kind of thing).

But though it be but one poem, what a poem it be! For his elegy must count as one of the most haunting evocations of our ultimate fate as any written in that melancholy, death-obsessed era. Using that favored Renaissance trope of antithesis, he movingly writes (being somewhere between the age of twenty-three and twenty-eight) that "My youth is gone, and yet I am but young."[3] New Critical orthodoxy would have us separate the circumstances of the elegy's composition from the poem itself, and yet it would be dishonest to say that some of the sublimity of Tichborne's lyric isn't in the fact that we envision him in a cold, unforgiving stone cell of the Tower desperately pressing pen to parchment as he attempts to get all of the words left within him out onto paper. But who really believes in that New Critical separation of context anymore anyhow?

Nobody would claim Tichborne to be the equivalent of a John Donne or George Herbert. And yet, is there not an incredible frankness that moves one equally when you remember that the poem which ends with "and now my life is done" was completed with the author's full knowledge that indeed within hours his life would be done? Tichborne, along with his fellow Elizabethan the Jesuit martyr Robert Southwell, offers a Western example of the Japanese poetic genre of the *jinsei*, that is, the poem written by one who is knowingly and shortly approaching their own death.[4] It is the genre that is best able to encapsulate what it means to hear a fly buzzing, to remind us that death may be abstract, but that it is also always particular. As a result, despite death's universality, it isn't really an abstraction to any of us. But, Jesus, Tichborne knew that score more than most.

I've been thinking about Tichborne recently, not because I am an expert on him (is anyone an expert on Chidiock Tichborne?) but because I couldn't help but contrast him to the transhumanist tech denizens profiled in Tad Friend's excellent April 3rd *New Yorker* article "The God Pill: Silicon Valley's quest for eternal life."[5] Friend interviews investors, scientists, and advocates for both the (obviously admirable) cause of life extension and the (delusional) one of technological immortality. He discusses both biological life-extension with the (weirdly appropriately named) English gerontologist Aubrey de Grey, and the technological Singularity with the seemingly brilliant but huckstery inventor Ray Kurzweil—whom I should mention before I appear too snarky, did manifestly improve the lives of millions with his invention of the Kurzweil Reading Machine.

But what emerges in Friend's piece is a collective portrait of tanned, toned, diet pill-popping, treadmill obsessed, emotionally stunted Silicon Valley technocrats who, not content to have altered everything about how we communicate and interact with human beings over the past generation, now have the arrogance to assume that they can easily "hack" death as well. Journalist and advocate for death with dignity, author Ann Neumann said in an interview with *America Magazine* that ours is a society "where death is hidden inside institutions."[6] Among the most privileged of our citizens, that invisibility of death in our culture is taken to its logical conclusion, by erasing the understanding that death even needs to exist. Last month in *Marginalia*, I wrote that in our current moment "awareness of death is as repressed [as] sex was to the Victorian," and what better example of repressing this awareness than the sanitized fantasy of dotcom millionaires and billionaires pretending that technological immortality is not just possible but likely?[7]

Mythically, it's a profoundly old story, the assumption that there is an easy material cure for death, traceable as far back as Gilgamesh confronting the immortal Utnapishtim and learning that death is indeed the mother of beauty. Figures in Friend's essay, like Peter Thiel and Jeff Bezos (neither of whom he interviews) come across with all the hubris of characters from Greek myth, as if inventing PayPal and writing checks to de Grey's Strategies for Engineered Negligible Senescence ensure that they can still that bell which tolls for them or brake the wheels on time's winged chariot. Friend quotes Arram Sabeti, founder of something called ZeroCater, who says, "The proposition that we can live forever is obvious. It doesn't violate the laws of physics, so we will achieve it," to which I respond with "Ask not for whom the heat death of the universe ultimately cools, it cools for thee." Sabeti's proclamation is a stunning bit of positivist hubris, not least of which because it's literally incorrect, for in the end, nobody and nothing, not even the universe, can escape the most poetic law of physics, the Second Law of Thermodynamics. But what does Tichborne have to do with Sabeti, or Google co-founder Sergey Brin, who sunnily tells an assembled party in Mandeville Canyon, Los Angeles, that "I'm not actually planning to die?" What does Tichborne, who perhaps melodramatically, but still honestly, wrote that he "sought my death and found it in my womb, / I looked for life and saw it was a shade, / I trod the earth and knew it was my tomb, / And now I die," have to do with Brin, who thinks that if he writes a big enough check he can bribe the Grim Reaper?

The difference between the assembled technological utopians and Tichborne is that, despite his melodramatic posturing, his romantic pose, and his at times overwrought verse, his approach to mortality was fundamentally more mature, and in his maturity, he conveyed a deep wisdom that de Grey, Kurzweil, and the rest of them lack. This maturity isn't because the techno-utopians believe in immortality and Tichborne didn't—far from it. Despite the fact that at no point in the elegy did Tichborne ever hint at anything concerning an afterlife, I have no doubt that as a staunch Catholic willing to be martyred, he firmly believed in a heavenly reward. Five years before his execution, Tichborne and his father narrowly escaped punishment for smuggling Catholic relics from the continent into Britain.[8] A man willing to risk decapitation for some bits of bone, rag, and wood is not wishy-washy, milquetoast, or agnostic when it comes to questions of fidelity. No, what made Tichborne more mature was his despairing honesty. What made Tichborne more mature is that he understood that he was going to die; he knew that whatever came next, the process itself wasn't an option or a choice. And he knew that fact, though he was on an abbreviated schedule; he knew that it's a fundamental truth for all of us—maybe the only universal and fundamental truth. What also made Tichborne more mature is the presumed basis for his trust in an afterlife, for in embracing religious justification for such a belief, I would argue he was on much more legitimate epistemological ground.

Do not mistake what I'm arguing; I am not claiming that supernatural life-after-death is "real" or not. I, of course, have absolutely no idea. Like most people aspiring to honesty, I'll admit that at some moments I'm sure that we're nothing but meat for vermiculation, and in the next, I'm certain that there is a transcendence that we're all promised to join, a world of light unto which we shall all ascend. Sometimes I have those contradictory feelings in the space of a few minutes. Except for those people that know neither the score nor the definitions, there are no atheists or theists, only an admixture of both. This isn't a claim for some personal superiority, merely an observation on the contingency of doubt since the dawn of modernity. But what I do know with certainty is that if there is to be true, genuine, eternal life, then there is no materialist explanation for such a possibility. That is not a dictate of theology, it is one of science, which the transhumanists abuse and make an idol out of so as to balm their fear of death.

Since Karl Popper's useful "falsification principle," it has been a philosophical matter of course to evaluate whether a proposition is scientific or not based on whether there is the possibility for said claim to be empirically falsified.[9] That is to say, can one envision an experimental or observational method by which a claim can be proven false? Note that the falsification principle can't verify the accuracy of a claim, only its status as a scientific one. So, as the famous example goes, the claim that "All swans are white" is a scientific claim, because whether correct or not it's possible to envision a situation in which the statement can be falsified, namely the discovery of a black swan. Now, a theological proposition such as the Filioque clause is one that can't be empirically falsified; it is epistemologically beyond measurement. No cyclotron can falsify either the Latin or Greek Church's positions on the issue of whether the Holy Spirit proceeds from the Father alone or also from the Son.

Some philosophers, historically the Vienna Circle logical positivists of the first few decades of the twentieth century to whom Popper was writing in reaction against, would argue that such theological claims (and indeed claims of aesthetics, metaphysics, myth, etc.) are logically meaningless. That may or may not be the case; of course, the great objection to such a "verification principle" (associated with the analytical philosopher Rudolf Carnap) is that the principle that the only legitimate statements are those that can be confirmed empirically is itself self-contradictory.[10] But I digress, my task is not to necessarily denigrate logical positivism as an epistemic system but rather to point out that religious claims about immortality, as they lay beyond the realm of Popperian falsification, are beliefs which epistemologically belong to a different category than do claims which could be empirically proven to be false.

And, the whole litany of transhumanist snake-oil chicanery, from the Robot Jesus of Kurzweil's Singularity, human consciousness downloaded to a computer hard-drive, cryogenic chambers, and visions of electronic immortality dancing in our heads, what of those? Well, those are claims about the material world, privy to potential falsification. And, unless I'm missing something, there is no physical process or law which can ensure the immortality of an individual human consciousness, none. Certainly life-extension is a possibility, and even if de Grey is correct that soon scientists will be able to ultimately extend human life-spans to a minimum of a millennium (though I'm dubious), that's just a more extreme version of good ol' fashioned life-extension facilitated by throwing out your cigarettes, pouring your tumbler of scotch down the drain, eating your spinach, looking both ways before you cross the street, and being the beneficiary of pure good luck. No, for eternity-eternity, as in forever-eternity, there can be no physical guarantee, only supernatural hope, for one once again comes upon that most poetic law of physics, which enshrines mortality in the dicta that all things must eventually tend toward sublime entropy.

In Friend's article, Martine Rothblatt, the CEO of a biotech firm with the distressingly ambiguous name of United Therapeutics matter-of-factly claims that "Clearly, it is possible, through technology, to make death optional." Clearly. Or not. I can't even keep the computer that I am writing this on from crashing. Clearly, it is possible through technology to extend life, and one would hope to also improve it. We know this is true because that's the history of modern medicine. Ideally, one would hope it's possible to extend and improve the lives of the largest number of people possible, and not just the millionaire anarcho-capitalists of Silicon Valley, but that's a political question for later. But Rothblatt isn't talking about modern medicine; she's talking about modern magic masquerading as medicine, for this isn't life extension but making death itself "optional." For some techno-utopians, this is the ultimate valediction of a certain libertarian-minded fetishizing of their god, the Invisible Hand, which becomes so powerful it can still Death itself.[11]

For the techno-utopian libertarian, late capitalism is late not because of the impending collapse of the market under its own excess but because eschatologically, what lies beyond is immortality purchased through check (or PayPal). In the fevered brain-in-a-vat imaginations of such transhumanists, death can become an option, like a choice of appetizers at a Palo Alto bistro or between seemingly identical shades of differing white paint you might pick for your glass-walled living room overlooking Big Sur. For Rothblatt is like Max von Sydow's knight in *The Seventh Seal*, except she is naïve enough to believe that she can pay Death to take a fall (if that term works for chess, but you get my point).[12] But the techno-utopian forgets that the house always, *always* wins. Peter Thiel, despite his worst intentions to enshrine inequality into the very nature of metaphysical reality, is thankfully, like all of us, mortal.

Death always has a way of coming to the programmer, no matter how plucky or optimistic. Because again, whether in flood or fire, in Big Freeze or Big Crunch, the universe must die, and so shall you. That is the dishonesty of the transhumanist promise—it has already failed the falsification test. By gambling for a materialist explanation for an afterlife, it has lost the race before the starter was even fired. Now, none of this means that religious versions of the afterlife are necessarily true or not (or what "true" even means in that context). But what it does mean is that theological explanations for immortality, in that they are epistemologically not under Popper's jurisdiction, are ones that can't be disproven empirically. A less complicated way of putting this is that heaven and hell may or may not be bullshit because it's impossible to know either way, but we know that totalizing transhumanist claims must ultimately be bullshit, for they come up against the very laws of physics which they claim undergird their plans.

In that sense, I see far more maturity in the religiously faithful, even (or maybe especially) those of an orthodox bent, because taking that leap of faith into the unknown valley is a more authentic and more honest approach to the universal tragedy of death than pretending that immortality lay in injecting yourself Elizabeth Bathory-style with the blood of healthy young people (seriously, in the article ...) or having a digitized version of your brain merge with the infinite interconnected Cloud which Kurzweil prophesizes will independently emerge by the year 2045. For that matter, an engaged and serious atheism, which rejects the possibility of the perseverance of identity after death, is also a more authentic and honest approach to extinction. My argument concerns not whether one should believe or disbelieve the metaphysical claims about an afterlife, only that believing in an afterlife for metaphysical reasons is more legitimate, and as a result more mature in its honesty than believing in heaven programed into a computer or resurrection facilitated by liquid nitrogen.

The chimeric mirage of physically finding an elixir for everlasting life is as old as Tithonus and as recent as Thiel. The motivation behind Gilgamesh searching for the boxthorn at the bottom of the sea and Ponce de Leon looking for the Fountain of Youth in Florida.[13] A very old potion in new test tubes, for transhumanism offers nothing novel, just a positivist religion written in the metaphysics of materialism, ironically, a philosophy that disproves the precepts of the cybernetic and cryogenic faith. What's telling is that from the Wandering Jew to Sir Galahad, immortality is never a prize, but always a curse.[14]

Tichborne may have bemoaned his early expiration date, but he didn't pine for wandering the Earth forever either, for again, his was a mature relationship to death. Lest I be too hard on the men and women interviewed in *The New Yorker* article, I should state that I clearly and deeply understand their desire—but I think the leap of faith into belief in religious immortality has the benefit of not being so easily disprovable as transhumanism.

But what do I know, who am I to talk about transhumanism being easily "disprovable?" It's true, I am a lowly literary scholar, no more well-versed in cybernetics, cryogenics, artificial intelligence, or uploading consciousness to a computer than any other educated reader perusing articles like Friend's—but can you begrudge me my skepticism? As a humanist, who has spent his adult life enmeshed in texts both canonical and not, texts from Ecclesiastes to Julian Barnes' brilliant *Nothing to Be Frightened Of*, works penned within the valley of the shadow of death, I know that no traveler has ever returned from that undiscovered country.[15] When Austrian roboticist Hans Moravec, a prominent transhumanist not mentioned in Friend's article, and a professor at my alma mater Carnegie Mellon University (though we've never met), says innocently that he has "already mentioned the possibility of [digitally] making copies of oneself, with each copy undergoing its own adventures" and that, as a result, "Concepts of life, death and identity will lose their present meaning," can one fault me for feeling that we've left the domain of science and entered that of a secularized religion, a positivist theology which enshrines technology as the engine of teleology?[16]

Moravec is a committed atheist (whose wife, fascinatingly enough, is an evangelical Christian), and yet despite his atheism, he seems unable to shed the traditional comforts of religion at its most basic.[17] Thiel, for his part, was raised as an evangelical Christian during his youth in Germany, and he claims to still be a religious

Christian (even appearing on a dais with Episcopalian theologian N.T. Wright).[18] But I wonder if in general, those techno-utopians, those transhumanists, are not largely composed of men (and to a lesser extent women) who have intuited that due to the insights of the scientific revolution that the supernatural promises of faith must be incorrect, but that they have personally not dealt with the implications of that supposed fact, and so they immaturely use the tools of positivist materialism to construct a new promise of immortality?

Barnes writes, "I don't believe in God, but I miss Him."[19] Kurzweil once said, "Does God exist? I would say 'Not yet.'"[20] Parse the difference, for the transhumanists push their religious anxiety to the point of deigning themselves gods and then patenting the afterlife. The difference, however, between a supernatural theology of the afterlife and Moravec's is that the former is not constrained by physical limitation; the metaphysical rules which define them are different from transhumanism's. Note that that doesn't mean they are correct, merely that they can't be dismissed in the same manner, because to critique them with the schema of materialism is to perform a category mistake. Transhumanism, on the other hand, is defined by materialism, a materialism that, by the very nature of physical law, means that ultimately the transhumanist promise itself must fail. British philosopher John Gray, one of the wittiest and most cognizant critics of the new immortality, writes, "transhumanism is not as rational as it seems ... Deriving from mystical philosophies such as Platonism and gnosticism, it is an idea at odds with scientific materialism."[21] But Platonism and Gnosticism both have the dignity to understand what they are, and not to masquerade as provable sciences. The promises of Christian resurrection may or may not be true, but they are promises that by their very definition are not of this world, and thus we must judge whether we believe them by a different criterion than that of Popper's falsification principle. But transhumanism? Well, I know for a fact that you can always unplug a computer. Or debug it of the ghost in the machine.

Not just as a humanist but also as a human, I am fully aware of that most precious wisdom which explains that "Sic transit gloria mundi." In our ever-continuing season of disciplinary mortality, humanists churn out copy concerning the utility of the humanities, with arguments normally running within the relatively narrow spectrum of appeals toward pragmatic utility (critical thinking!) to mealy-mouthed, rapturous canonicity (the Great Books!). Here is what I think is a novel argument to inject into that discussion—the humanities provide the wisdom that reminds you that you too shall die. If all of culture, all of art, all of literature, indeed all of religion is one great reaction toward that most fundamental of truths, then the transhumanist promise is just one more bit of denialism that pretends that mortality is a problem to be simply solved by human ingenuity.

Montaigne said that "to study philosophy is to learn to die."[22] Peter Thiel disagrees; he doesn't like academics or college much; no doubt he rejects most philosophy as only so much navel-gazing (in spite of, or perhaps because of, a B.A. in philosophy from Stanford).[23] Far more practical to envision Randian utopias floating as constructed islands on the Pacific or eternity as organized on the circuit boards of an artificially intelligent supercomputer. He would do well to put a statue of himself amongst the sands of Silicon Valley with the admonition that we should "Look on my works, ye Mighty, and despair!"[24] But, might I humbly suggest that the immature rejection of such a basic fact as one's own death robs one of life before it has even ended? For in rejecting the very idea of death, we by necessity reject the idea of the good death, of the *Ars moriendi*. This is a dangerous road to traverse, and ironically, the fantasies of Silicon Valley, and the tremendous accumulation of capital which they represent, indicate a deeper malignancy in our body politic.

While Peter Thiel's friends dream of electronic immortality, the president whom he advises oversees the dismantling of our healthcare system and the condemnation of 24 million Americans who will lose their insurance. Transhumanists attend TED talks about how death for them is "optional," while advocating for a system that denies the poor based on "pre-existing conditions," and so we witness the new eugenicist doublethink logic of a type of genocide. Death is inevitable to all, but the myopia and narcissism that allows the uber-rich to pretend that they alone can escape it while denying others the medical care that we know we are capable of as a society have very real implications. Death might be inevitable, but a good death is sadly not. The first is the purview of God and nothing can be done about it, the latter is the purview of humans and we have a responsibility to try and benefit as many as possible with the dignity of the *Ars moriendi*. Transhumanism, far from being a regenerative imaginative worldview, is one that is moribund to the core; it suffers from a profound lack of creativity in terms of restructuring social organization, preferring instead to masturbate to thoughts of a mythic lifeboat from death, reserved for the very rich. It's an obscenity. Again, if humanism has any wisdom to impart against the machinations and mirages of theologized techno-utopianism, it's that old adage that "This too shall pass." Perhaps, as with the Roman generals of old, men like Thiel (or he whom the entrepreneur endorsed for president) would do well to have an assistant at their side, periodically whispering in their ear, "Respice post te. Hominem te memento." That is "Look after you and remember that you are a man," whether you've taken your ninety vitamin supplements or put your head on ice or not.[25]

Kurzweil says, "It's a common philosophical position that death gives meaning to life, but death is a great robber of meaning … It robs us of love. It is a complete loss of ourselves. It is a tragedy."[26] Kurzweil is wrong, but for understandable reasons. Death is most certainly a tragedy; to paraphrase Donne, the loss of any human diminishes us all. And the fact that death is intrinsic to life, well, that's by definition one of the most unfair things that is conceivable. Where Kurzweil errs in thinking that death being a tragedy means that it becomes a "robber of meaning," for nothing about the nature of tragedy necessarily implies meaninglessness. Again, don't mistake what I'm saying. Nothing is more insulting in its triteness than consoling those left behind with the cheap adage that God must have had his reasons. Rather, I am arguing that death in and of itself neither implies meaning nor meaninglessness, but rather it is the job of the living to endow life with meaning. The sentiment is less a rebuke to a worldview like Kurzweil's and more of a promise, or even a consolation to one who fears that death means the end of meaning—which is all of us sometimes. And meaning is what defines numinous experience, for religion has always had meaning at its core and not just the opiate comforts of immortality. Religion seeks to endow the profane with the charged electricity of the sacred, whether we're to individually survive or not. What faith at its fullest expression promises, whether through "Carpe Diem" or "Memento Mori," is not necessarily the existence of life after death but rather how to live your life with such beauty, justice, truth, and love that it doesn't matter whether life continues after death or not.

I do not wish to be callous, but as death is our common fate (whether the party in the article acknowledges that or not), I feel like I have a stake in such questions and can render my judgment. I understand the fear that motivates the transhumanist perspective, for I am human and let nothing that is post-human be alien to me—and what is more human than to fear death? And not just the process, but also the possibility of nothingness itself. Our old friend Tichborne, in a different poem, this one to his old friend Anthony Babington who got him into that whole mess in the first place, sweetly writes that God "shall remove our grounded ship far from this dangerous place, ... And keep ourselves on land secure, ... Sweet friend, till then content thy self." Who doesn't pray for some secure destination away from this dangerous place of life, some field on the other side of true and false where we may once again see those whom we have loved, and love still?

Kurzweil explains how he lost his father at a relatively young age, as indeed many of the transhumanists have, indeed as I did as well. Friend writes that Kurzweil "hopes to someday create a virtual avatar of his father and then populate the doppelgänger's mind with all this information, as well as with his own memories of and dreams about his father, exhuming a Fredric Kurzweil 2.0." His hope is understandable, even poignant, but it is also unspeakably sad, for it appears to be much more of a delusion than those dusty desert promises of religious faith that the sophisticated maintain have been roundly rejected. I do not suggest that faith comes easily, or that we want to have a cheap faith— no, a faith worth anything must be very expensive. I ask not to trade the delusions of technocratic fundamentalism for those of a primitive religious faith, but I do believe that, however uncomfortably, we can dwell in contradiction, for in that ambiguity there is always hope. Perhaps my father and I shall meet again, but I hope that it would not be on a hard drive.

I contrast Kurzweil's hologram with something said by the children's book author Maurice Sendak, who discussed the death of his beloved brother Jack with the NPR interviewer Terry Gross. Like Kurzweil, and de Grey, and Moravec, and the others, Sendak couldn't reconcile himself to traditional religious faith. He told Gross that "When [people] die they're out of my life, they're gone forever," but he continued, "I still fully expect to see my brother again."[27] There is a beauty in that view of mortality, having shuffled off certainty with our bodily coil, finding more hope in a paradoxical promise than in that old myth that eternal life can be found just around the corner, or in some exotic land, or in some alchemist's elixir. Such a perspective is beautiful not in spite of the doubt at its center but because of it. Such a perspective has a particular kind of truth precisely because of that doubt. Such a perspective is the very essence of genuine faith.

Part Four

A Pale Horse

9

On Literature and the Anthropocene

Part One: Writing for Memory

Pangea's expanse, stretching along the equator and encircled by a shallow super ocean, was punctuated by dense and tall forests.[1] The continent's spindly trees reached up toward the cool, oxygen-rich atmosphere, the sky a deep, celestial blue, sulfate ash from volcanoes staining the sunsets orange and lavender. Forests from the shoals of the Panthalassa Ocean to the shores of the Paleo-Tethys Sea, along the spine of the Central Pangean Mountains to the massive peaks of the Appalachians, not yet winnowed down by friction into green rolling hills. Now extinct *lepidodendron* and *sigillaria* trees were packed together, the forest floor a lattice-work of exposed root systems, the trunks of these massive plants engirted with bark, branches of ferns widely spread.[2] Among the mangroves scattered along the coasts was a vast ecosystem of creatures, massive arthropods and insects drunk on the oxygenated air, who contested with amphibians that were meters long, all shaded in the dark solitude of this primeval arboretum, the air an orchestra of whirring from giant dragonflies, the clicking of gargantuan spiders.

When trees died, collapsed under their own weight, they would pile atop each other, their fibrous wood too sinewy for any bacterium or fungus to digest. Today, a felled stump is marked by the lurid red and corpuscular purple bloom of mushrooms, transforming wood into a piquant, sludgy hummus, but 300 million years ago, it was impossible for dead forests to rot.[3] Brittle timber stacked atop itself, pressed down and ossified, until over the eons it converted into peat and bitumen, anthracite and lignite. Eventually, fungi and bacteria would evolve that would break down these remains, but not before these ancient forests were victimized by their own supremacy. Having radiated so much oxygen, temperatures eventually plummeted, causing mass extinction, what geologists call a "minor" event, of which there have been many in the Earth's some 6 billion years. Currently, we're in the midst of the sixth major extinction event—it will be multitudes greater in damage than the Carboniferous Rainforest Collapse.[4]

"Carboniferous," incidentally, for the most salient element of that epoch, substance of coal and diamonds, allotropic atom of life. Each of the Carboniferous' subdivisions is named after where the cemeteries of those trees would be unearthed—*Muscovian, Kasimovian, Mississippian, Pennsylvanian*. West Virginia and Wales once kissed, evidence in the veins of black coal underneath the skin of the planet like a cancerous tumor, or maybe graphite scratched across the page. Carbon is, as chemist Primo Levi described it in *The Periodic Table*, the most narrative element. "I could recount an endless number of stories about carbon atoms that become colors or perfumes in flowers," writes Levi, "of others which, from tiny algae to small crustaceans to fish, gradually return as carbon dioxide to the waters of the sea, in a perpetual, frightening round-dance of life and death, in which every devourer is immediately devoured."[5] Today, our geologic era is named after ourselves—the Anthropocene. Understandable, but it doesn't convey the rapaciousness, the hunger, the avarice which drives our frenzied and cannibalistic madness, the depletion of the earth. More appropriate to call our moment "The Devouring."

As with the long disappeared *sigalaria* and *lepidodendron*, carbon imprisoned within their fossilized bodies, exorcized through an ecstasy of burning, foolish men unaware of those hidden specters and their latent revenge. Novelist Pitchaya Sudbanthad describes this sacrificial immolation in his essay for the Amy Brady and Tajja Isen anthology *The World as We Knew It: Dispatches from a Changing Climate*, writing that the "empire of capital would not let the dead, ancient animals alone. Through systemized extraction, they were being unearthed to light up and power our cars, motorcycles, and sky-shattering jets, and they were vengeful at us for disturbing our rest."[6] Any reader of gothic horror knows that ghosts cannot be disturbed, their slumber always finite, even if for millions of years. "The dead want to quicken our union with them," writes Sudbanthad, "so that we may sooner know what it is like to be exhumed for some living being's expedient use."

All of these authors are confronted with the same collective *memento mori* issue which any conscious being must ask in this hazy dusk. *How do we mark all of that which we've lost, all of that which we're in the midst of losing? What purpose does putting one word after another have anymore? Who will survive to read us, to remember us when everything else is gone?* Pieter Vermeulen in *Literature and the Anthropocene* compares this variety of "Ecological grief," with its "feelings of anger, powerlessness, and depression in the face of an ongoing or anticipated destruction of the lifeworlds that sustain us," to philosopher Glenn Albrecht's concept of "solastagia." This neologism, Vermeulen explains, encompasses the "psychological pain experienced when one's sense of belonging is undone by environmental change," contrary to nostalgia where "*staying* home makes you sick because the place that was once home is being destroyed before your very eyes."[7] A variation of this inquiry must haunt anyone in these days of super hurricanes and massive wildfires, of pandemics and climate refugees. Our apocalypse is coming—has come—in a billion little incidences of acidified waters and drowned cities, for nobody has ever before experienced the desertification of a planet, the erasure of all civilization. "The tether between what is and what used to be, constantly stretching under the weight of history and progress, will not stretch any more. It will snap," writes Omar El Akkad.[8]

We see the evidence in that liturgy of small things now mute—in dead birds and silent insects; and the large things now roaring—the derechos and tornadoes, hurricanes and heatwaves. A short brief of individual griefs. Few of us can grapple with the implications of an increase of carbon dioxide in parts per million, other than that it means rising temperatures, rising oceans, rising misfortunes. We can remember stark changes and dark omens within our own lifetimes, with Brady and Isen noting that we are in a "time when the majority of us can still remember when things were more stable … We are forced to confront, in strange and sometimes painful ways, how much those places have changed."[9] A harrowing litany—the heat-death of majestic saguaro cacti in the Sonoran Desert and of Lyme-carrying tick infestation in Cape Cod, of New Hampshire's White Mountains without snow, and Dominica demolished by hurricanes. These are topics that must be analyzed through science, but they must also be approached through poetry. Adam Trexler in *Anthropocene Fictions: The Novel in a Time of Climate Change* writes that literature "can describe these patterns without reducing their complexity to a monovocal account, a set of bare 'interests,' an immovable orthodoxy, or a predetermined certainty."[10] Literature can be at home with negative capability, that domain in which the subtlety and nuance of humanity are best expressed.

So, give expression to all that has been lost, and all that is yet to be lost. The winters without snow and the endless summer heatwaves, how essayist Gabrielle Bellot describes it as being "as if a star's brightness in our sky had slowly shifted, night after night, until we came to believe, astronomy notwithstanding, that it had always been that intense."[11] The changes of the seasons as if counting the rosary for me, the regularity of their shifts almost a ritual, though now the months are unpredictable, out of sync. "There is so much to mourn that sometimes it's hard to discern from where my sadness springs, or to what it belongs," writes Melissa Febos.[12] Autumn on the Pennsylvania Turnpike, that bushel of yellow, and orange, and red; stopping at the Sideling Hill farmer's market for Amish shoofly pie, clouds of respiration visible in dawn's chill. Now, the trees are scraggly brown, torrid days stretching into early October. Winter flakes, fat and slow, falling over a December sidewalk and burying it in the white, holy silence of blankness, red, orange, and yellow of Christmas light reflecting off the mirrored surface. Ten years ago, Christmas was so warm that we opened our presents on the porch. Spring was when our magnolia tree would erupt in its haze of purple and white, but recently warm weather has tricked her into awakening too early, only to be stunted by the return of frost. Summer, of saltwater wind and waving arms out of car windows, rhythm of cicada and fireflies, their glow growing dimmer as the heat becomes more uncomfortable, until it can't be tolerated at all.

"We are to lose so much," writes El Akkad, "climate change is going to render our past as unrecognizable as our future."[13] As children, they told us we had centuries; later, that there would be decades, recently it feels like years, sometimes like a few months. Through all of that, writing seems pathological. "I have made a monument more lasting than bronze," the ancient Roman poet Horace said, but what good is print when all the paper is to pulp, a humid and sticky mess in a quiet world after the average temperature has risen more than eight degrees Fahrenheit and the whole biodome has collapsed?[14] Even a bronze would be meaningless on an empty planet. As the Anthropocene ends, there are still reasons to write—to preserve, to understand, even to indict. Warning, it might be assumed by some, is pointless. All of those who are responsible are dead or so rich that the heat will touch them last. They already know what they did. Preservation, the recording of myths and poems, stories and songs, is at least redemptive. El Akkad argues that "We have an obligation to document and preserve ... these stories we tell ourselves. We have an obligation to do it now."[15] Visualizing readers on the other side, after Amsterdam, Venice, and New York have been devoured, when the southwest is uninhabitable and the ice caps have all melted, at least staves off total despair. Ultimately, though, I write for myself. During the Anthropocene, I write to understand as this devouring happens. I write to mourn as it happens. I write to bear witness, even if only to myself.

"I want to believe that, even if there is no grand meaning for our lives and our planet has a finite lifespan—as do our art and dreams—that art is worth making and love is worth finding," Bellot writes, and I agree.[16] Writing is sanctified because it's a ritual of meaning in the happening, and sometimes there is a grace powerful enough that somebody gets consolation from that act when a human reads and hopefully encounters another. Words and narratives matter as much as they ever did, for if they mean everything to an individual, it doesn't matter if they mean nothing to everybody else. "Ten thousand years of living in a steady climate is over. We have returned to the times of mythology, and we need new stories to survive," writes Meera Subramanian, and I also agree with her.[17] What form these stories will take, how they will be preserved, who shall tell these stories—I don't know. But the why of them always makes sense. Humans tell stories because we're storytelling creatures. Tautological, yes. Still, meaning endures in memory, so we carry with us those cool autumns and warm springs. If the real bronze has long since melted, we can hopefully craft a monument somehow enduring, even if it's not the original, and we can pray that we have great-grandchildren who are able to imagine it.

Part Two: Writing for Protest

Though it's more than a hundred miles from the coast, during the early evening of October 29, 2012, my apartment in Bethlehem, Pennsylvania, had the salty odor of the shore. In the dwindling light before Hurricane Sandy smashed into Jersey and New York, so much sea moisture had descended on our landlocked town that it smelled like the Atlantic City Boardwalk. Something foreboding about that during the proverbial calm before the storm, reminding me of the passage from Zora Neal Hurston's novel that gave it its title, when Janie and Tea Cake huddled together as the eye of a hurricane passed over and she described "their eyes straining against crude walls and their souls asking if He meant to measure their puny might against His. They seemed to be staring at the dark, but their eyes were watching God."[18]

On that howling night that would knock out power in Bethlehem for close to a week, I had no sense that I was watching God. Rather, I was spooked by the incongruity of that beachy smell, the sense described by Roy Scranton in his collection *We're Doomed. Now What?: Essays on War and Climate Change* that "nothing feels right, not the land, not the weather."[19] If Hurston's characters were looking at God, then I felt like I was looking at something strangely more terrifying—humanity's hubris altering the seasons. Ursula K. Heise in *Imagining Extinction: The Cultural Meanings of Endangered Species* writes that "In our own historical moment, the environmentalist rhetoric of decline has come to a head in the cultural meme of the end of nature, the idea that nature such as we have understood it since the Romantic age has disappeared," but more than an ending what I detect is a revision.[20] For this is what the Anthropocene portends—an inverted sublimity. Ecological collapse, along with the potential of nuclear Armageddon, signals the first time in the three millennia since the prophet Daniel had his apocalyptic nightmares that humanity's end is conceivable by our own hand, what Scranton describes as the "beginning of the end of civilization as we know it," where "Not one of us is innocent, not one of us is safe."[21] Oceans swallow Venice and Amsterdam, Paradise California is immolated and Manhattan's subways flood, and we can meditate on humanity's cracked grandeur.

Scranton considers what the Anthropocene means for the humanities, though he doesn't have much sympathy for "literature scholars using the Anthropocene as a new way to talk about trees in Milton."[22] He is impatient with the mining of climate apocalypse as just another fashionable theory, something used to pad CVs and get tenure publications. "I love trees. I love Milton. But is this the best we can do?" he asks. For Scranton, grappling with the Anthropocene isn't like faddish Darwinian criticism or the digital humanities; it entails asking what it means to live nearing the end of days, to live "in the fall … in the long dim days of decline and collapse and retrenchment and violence and confusion and sorrow and endless, depthless, unassuageable human suffering."[23] The polysyndeton, the parallelism, and the theological vocabulary indicates what Scranton is up to. It's not to form a panel for the MLA; it's to pen a missive from Armageddon (not that those are mutually exclusive).

More appropriate to categorize Scranton as the literary critical arm of the speculative realists, philosophers like Timothy Morton, Jane Bennett, and Quintin Meillassoux with their calls for an "object-oriented ontology," as when Scranton implores us to not just see environmental issues with human eyes but with "golden-cheeked warbler eyes, coho salmon eyes, and polar bear eyes ... with the wild, barely articulate being of clouds and seas and rocks and trees and stars."[24] This is no woolly pantheism. Scranton's mysticism is as all true mysticisms should be—cold and hard. Scranton could be grouped with the British novelist Paul Kingsnorth's Dark Mountain Project. Both Scranton and Kingsnorth, as well as the other writers with the Dark Mountain Project, share a perspective that could be termed "eco-pessimism." As is made clear throughout *We're Doomed. Now What?* (not least of which with the title) Scranton believes that not only is climate change bad, but that it's much worse than you might suppose.

With grim fatalism, he writes that the "planet *will* get warmer. The ice caps *will* melt. The seas *will* rise."[25] He rightly castigates the selfish myopia of "Right-wing denialists [who] insist that climate change isn't happening," but also the sunny optimism of "left-wing denialists" that insist our "problems are fixable." Nor does he curry favor with the techno-utopians who "argue that more technology is the answer" or "Incrementalists" who "keep trusting the same institutions and leaders that have been failing us for decades."[26] In the *New Left Review*, Frederic Jameson argued that it is "easier to imagine the end of the world than to imagine the end of capitalism."[27] *We're Doomed. Now What?* is a protracted exploration of exactly what this means. To imagine apocalypse *because* of capitalism. *We're Doomed. Now What?* asks us what it means to be the last (or the second-to-last) generation of humans because of our avarice.

Scranton writes that "We all see what's happening, we read it in the headlines every day, but seeing isn't believing, and believing isn't accepting. We respond according to our prejudices, acting out of instinct, reflex, and training."[28] To make the connection between unseasonably warm days and an abstract diagram charting rising temperatures correlated to industrial carbon dioxide output requires, in some sense, an imagination that we still collectively lack. Poetically, Scranton writes that there's a "time lag between CO2 increase and subsequent effects, between the wind we sow and the whirlwind we reap. Our lives are lived in that gap."[29] Our lives, I'll add, are in the hour before the storm hits.

Before a hurricane, there is an eeriness as birds depart and animals hide. As mega-storms batter Puerto Rico and Houston, as New England autumns now regularly have days that reach temperatures into the 80s, as California burns, we see our planet's equivalent. An increasing dissipation of any calm before the storm. Reading the United Nations Intergovernmental Panel Report on Climate Change, or the fourth National Climate Assessment, with their data about future human extinction, is like watching the birds fly away before a hurricane. Truly an era in which the seals have been broken and there is silence in the heavens, as Scranton reflects that "we might wish we could take Nietzsche's place. He had to cope only with the death of God ... while we must come to terms with the death of our whole world."[30] From our *Götterdämmerung*, I have one indelible image of the night that Sandy whipped its winds down through the Lehigh Valley. Rain lashed horizontally at windows which barely held, the horizon lit green with transponder explosions, the storm so all permeating that everything seemed as if water, the hulking rusted corpse of the steel mill now completely obscured by the storm. I spent that evening illuminated only by votive candles purchased at a bodega, listening to the wind, wearing a head-strap with a flashlight affixed to it so as to read a post-apocalyptic novel in the darkness. Perhaps I was clued into our collective unconsciousness, aware of our impending extinction. I never finished that book.

As another factum for the apocalyptic brief, I'll reiterate the opening of presents outside on Christmas morning 2015—in Pittsburgh. Or the recent deafening silence of insects in late summer. And the smell of burning California in the streets of New York. Scranton writes that the "catastrophe is *now*, even if it's impossible for most of us to see that fact through the blinders of day-to-day time."[31] Hard to immediately connect saltwater air in a landlocked city to climate change, for as Scranton notes:

> it's cognitively almost impossible to keep in mind the intricate relationships that tie together an oil well in Venezuela, Siberian permafrost, Saudi F-15s bombing a Yemeni wedding, subsidence along the Jersey Shore, albedo effect near Kangerlussuaq, the Pacific Decadal Oscillation, the polar vortex, shampoo, California cattle, the Great Pacific Garbage Patch, leukemia, plastic, paper, the Sixth Extinction, Zika, and the basic decisions we make every day, are forced to make every day, in a world we didn't choose but were thrown into.[32]

It's not that the science is complex (though it is, albeit easy to simplify for lay people), but rather that we're so enmeshed within dominant ideologies that we are dissuaded from noticing how often we can wear short sleeves in December.

Much of the critic Mark Fisher here, though "capitalist realism" never appears by name in *We're Doomed. Now What?*[33] Paralleling Fisher, Scranton writes that responding to climate change is like "responding to capitalism, or society, or the atmosphere. It is our environment. It is our world."[34] We're like the apocryphal Australian aborigines of legend, so embedded within their environment that they were literally unable to see Cook's ships as they sailed into Botany Bay. Fisher's concept of capitalist realism, owing much to Jameson, was a trenchant analysis of how it really is easier to imagine the end of the world before the end of Exxon.

Fisher asked if capitalism is "so seamless, and if current forms of resistance are so hopeless and impotent, where can an effective challenge come from?"[35] If you're an eco-pessimist, the answer is negative. Rightly condemning the secularized Puritanism embodied by trendy, eco-individualist liberalism, Scranton explains that even "if millions suddenly went vegan, swore off airplanes, sold their cars, and had themselves sterilized, it wouldn't significantly slow down global warming."[36] More than just the gallows glee of a Buddhist who enjoys meat (as he describes himself), Scranton makes the important point that the moralizing language of personal responsibility is completely inadequate to actually stop our looming apocalypse. *It isn't your personal responsibility, and you can't individually solve it*—so while you should probably recycle, there's little need to put on a hair shirt and cincture if you don't. Even more importantly, the market-obsessed language of commercial solutions is almost comically inadequate to the enormity of the challenge, where recycling or opting to purchase an electric vehicle is all that needs to be done to save the planet. Neoliberalism has no regenerative power in it—it can't cure itself, much less the world.

But Scranton doesn't hold out much hope for the required massive political, economic, and cultural solutions either. He writes that "Anyone who pays much attention to politics can assume that we're almost certainly going to botch this challenge," and anyone aware that since 2000 we've been saddled with two of the worst presidents in U.S. history because they won through the unfair and irrational stipulations of the Electoral College while losing the popular vote all because we fetishize an eighteenth-century document meant to reify the power of the landed class and slave owners can't help but concur with Scranton's pessimism.[37] When Scranton contends that it's "probably already too late to stop it, even if the world's political and economic elites were willing and able to radically transform our global fossil-fueled economy which they're not," is it possible to disagree with him using anything other than blind optimistic faith? Doesn't such sunny anodyne positivity sound sort of moronic? Our global position is fucked, where from Beijing to Brasilia we're "incapable of exerting the rational collective will necessary to save our civilization from destruction," rather finding "ourselves reduced to something less than human, lacking even the dumb instinct for survival we see in plants."[38] Such is the nature of Scranton's eco-pessimism that he reads the data with a sober mind and decides that it's unlikely any environmental *deus ex machina* is coming, so better to prepare ourselves for that inevitability like a Stoic awaiting death.

Except that the death we're waiting for isn't just individual, it's that of the entire human species. Scranton writes that the "Anthropocene is an apocalypse, but an apocalypse that's already been revealed and is already happening, though not all at once and not all the same."[39] Illuminating to consider this from the standpoint of eschatology, behooving us to consider the full implications of apocalyptic language, even if we're to read it as metaphorical. In fact, it's crucial to read Scranton's point as metaphorical, for though climate change may signal any number of hideous things, it isn't literally an apocalypse that is "already happening." Our ability to still write, ponder, and reflect on these ideas is all the evidence needed to point out that the *eschaton* has yet to be immanentized by carbon dioxide in our atmosphere. German poet Hans Magnus Enzensberger writes in a 1978 issue of the *New Left Review* that apocalypse is "ever present, but never 'actual' … an image that we can construct for ourselves, an incessant production of our fantasy, the catastrophe in the mind."[40] Armageddon is like death; easy to endlessly imagine, but by its very definition, impossible to understand, as none of us has experienced either. Such was a point made by Jacques Derrida in a 1984 issue of *Diacritics*, when he wrote that apocalypse must imply "irreversible destruction, leaving no traces of the ... basis of literature."[41] Derrida's point cuts to the fundamental oxymoron at the core of "post-apocalyptic literature." Such a literal genre would be an impossibility, for if you can still write, then it isn't yet the apocalypse.

Apocalypse is a specifically religious concept, the unveiling at the end of time which either inaugurates or terminates the millennium. Since the advent of the nuclear era, it's certainly come to be associated with societal or environmental collapse, but it does bear repeating that such scenarios are technically not "the Apocalypse" proper. While trying to avoid sounding like the internet comment complaining that an author is misusing the word "decimate," I do think it's fair to say that "apocalypse as metaphor" in reference to collapse could be applied to any number of historical incidents, from the Ostrogoths sacking Rome to the Easter Islanders descending into cannibalism. "Apocalypse" happens a lot, even if the current one we're facing could be the final one. This may seem to be mere quibbling—what difference does it make as Antarctic ice shelves fall into the sea if that doesn't herald the actual trumpets of Revelation? But we can't forget the connotations of the metaphors which we choose to use, even the good ones.

I think it makes sense to isolate the specific models of apocalypse offered as metaphors in *We're Doomed. Now What?* In Christian eschatology, scholars normally divide apocalyptic perspective into two broad categorizations, that of pre-millennial and post-millennial theories (among others). The former refers to the position that apocalypse must occur before Christ's millennial rule on Earth, the latter that apocalypse occurs after. Pre-millennialism is ultimately a despairing theology, adherents waiting for the intercession of apocalypse to upend inequities. Post-millennialism holds out the possibility of progress to perfection built by human efforts, heralding the ultimate arrival of Christ as a result.[42] In secularized form (and all secular ideas are simply theology wearing a mask), Scranton seems to oscillate between these positions. Sometimes an optimistic post-millennialist who believes that radical change could stave off apocalypse, when Scranton writes that of the radical reorientation of "all human economic and social production," but then the pessimistic pre-millennialist understanding that this is a "task that is scarcely imaginable, much less feasible."[43]

Which metaphor we choose, which model of apocalypse we turn toward, has policy implications. Scranton rightly fingers neoliberal late capitalism as that which has brought us to the precipice, noting that "realistically, making human life sustainable at this point would demand a socialist revolution."[44] The question is, will millennium happen before most of the world has to die, or does that utopia await us after the catastrophe? Or will there be no millennium, only Judgement Day? *We're Doomed. Now What?* offers no prediction, but how could any one of us know what this looks like? Science fiction novelist Ursula K. LeGuin offered a helpful reminder, noting that "We live in capitalism. Its power seems inescapable. So did the divine right of kings."[45] Indeed, if we understand the Anthropocene as "apocalyptic" in a theological sense, then the resultant eschaton is a rupture in history, something which allows for the countenancing of alternative ways of being, of consideration about how we might reorganize how we do things. Timothy Clark in *Ecocriticism on the Edge: The Anthropocene as a Threshold Concept* admits that this period may signal not only despair but something all the more surprising—hope. He writes that the "Anthropocene is both frightening and intellectual liberating ... [because the] breakdowns of inherited demarcations of thought can still become a means of disclosure and revision."[46]

Similarly, Scranton, the post-millennialist writes, "We need to work together to transform a global order of meaning focused on accumulation into a new order ... that knows the value of limits, transience, and restraint."[47] Hard to imagine this future where spiritually we've founded "a world religion that worshiped Mother Earth and put harmony with nature over all other values," but why not dare to imagine it?[48] Our future, our survival, depends on the complete uprooting and reorientation of all such values. If apocalypse is truly an "unveiling" in this original sense, why not let this be its significance in the present? Drawing from science fiction author Octavia Butler's imagined "Earthseed" religion from her novel *Parable of the Sower*, Monika Kaup in *New Ecological Realisms: Post-Apocalyptic Fiction and Contemporary Theory* argues that we can create "a metaphysic of survival founded on the facticity of catastrophe ... A metaphysic of contingency emerging from the experience of disaster, it turns the devastating fact of destruction into a positive principle on which to found post-apocalyptic survival."[49] If the spread of a new global perspective, a new pantheistic and humanistic theology to fix the ruptures caused by capitalism seems unlikely, consider that Christianity went from a persecuted minority to an imperial religion in three centuries; that Muhammad conquered the entire Arabian Peninsula in a lifetime. And neither Paul nor Muhammad had social media!

If the disjunctions of our current crack-up have instructed us in anything, it's how fast ideologies can spread—nothing says that they must always be poisonous ones. The Iraqi poet Naseer Hassan tells Scranton that "Hopelessness is the limit and beginning of a new kind of hope ... Hopelessness makes possible a new hope that is more than a faith in the basic tissue of life that is stronger than any disaster. This is how humanity survives. This is the strength that keeps us going."⁵⁰ As temperatures rise, as the ice caps encompass less of the planet, let us commit ourselves to building that new world, even if it must be constructed atop the shallow remains of our coastal cities and in howling deserts, for we may have no choice.

Part Three: Writing for Meaning

Hard not to see the coming collapse as of late. Journalist David Wallace-Wells puts it succinctly in a landmark piece about climate change which appeared in *New York Magazine* in 2017: "It is, I promise, worse than you think."⁵¹ Weather patterns that would have seemed apocalyptic but a generation ago—frequent hurricanes, wildfires, heat waves—are now regular. Every summer seemingly sees the worst heat waves in history until the next summer. At *The New Republic*, philosopher Alexis Papazoglou opines that there is an argument which could be made that "bringing children into a decaying world, without even the opportunity to do something about it, seems a cruel fate to inflict on someone, especially your own child."⁵² Novelist Jonathan Franzen, in a controversial piece for *The New Yorker*, wrote that "you have a good chance of witnessing the radical destabilization of life on earth—massive crop failures, apocalyptic fires, imploding economies, epic flooding, hundreds of millions of refugees fleeing regions made uninhabitable … If you're under thirty, you're all but guaranteed to witness it."⁵³ Facing the reality of such a situation, despair hardly seems an irrational emotion.

In such a world, it's no wonder that people despair. Psychoanalyst and Holocaust survivor Viktor Frankl presciently describes such sentiments in his 1946 classic *Man's Search for Meaning*. Frankl describes something that "so many patients complain [about] today, namely, the feeling of the total and ultimate meaninglessness of their lives."[54] Staring down the apocalypse, suddenly a cracked kind of nihilistic wisdom emerges justifying disparate phenomena of our era, from addiction to belief in pseudo-scientific theories, for in Frankl's analysis, an "abnormal reaction to an abnormal situation is normal behavior."[55] When scientists worry that humanity is facing extinction, we can agree that ours is very much an abnormal situation.[56]

Which is why *Man's Search for Meaning* is perhaps the work to return to in our humid days of the Anthropocene, the geological epoch in which we currently live, defined by our detrimental shaping of the natural world. Already a successful psychotherapist in Vienna before he was sent to Auschwitz (later being transferred to Dachau, among other concentration camps), Frankl was part of what's known as the Third Wave of psychoanalysis.[57] Reacting against both Sigmund Freud and Alfred Adler, Frankl rejected the first's theories concerning the "will to pleasure" and the latter's "will to power." By contrast, Frankl writes that "Man's search for meaning is the primary motivation in his life and not a 'secondary rationalization' of instinctual drives."[58]

Where a Freudian might see culture as a byproduct of our sexual urges, and Adler understanding it as a force used to dominate others, Frankl argued that literature, art, religion, and all of the other cultural phenomenon that place meaning at their core are things-unto-themselves, and furthermore are the very basis for how we find purpose. In private practice, Frankl developed a methodology called "logotherapy," describing it as defined by the fact that "striving to find a meaning in one's life is the primary motivational force in man."[59] For Frankl, there was much that humanity can live without, but if we're devoid of a sense of purpose and meaning, then we ensure our eventual demise.

In Vienna, he was Dr. Viktor Frankl, head of the neurology department of the Rothschild Hospital, but in Auschwitz, he was only "number 119,104."[60] For Frankl, the concentration camp was the very null point of meaning, a type of absolute zero for purpose in life. Already having developed his theories about logotherapy, Frankl smuggled a manuscript of the book he was working on into the camp, only to lose it and be forced to recreate it from memory upon liberation. While in Auschwitz, he informally worked as a physician, finding that acting as an analyst to his fellow prisoners gave him a purpose that aided in his own survival, even as he ostensibly was assisting others. In discussions with those men, he came to certain conclusions that bolstered his hypothesis that would later become foundational in the nascent field of humanistic psychology. One was that the "prisoner who had lost faith in the future—his future—was doomed."[61] Frankl recounts how that even in the camps, where suicide was understandably endemic, the prisoners who seemed to have the best chance of survival were not necessarily those who were the strongest, or those who were the physically healthiest, but those somehow capable of directing their thoughts toward a sense of meaning. A few prisoners were "able to retreat from their terrible surroundings to a life of inner riches and spiritual freedom," and in the imagination of such a space, there was the potential for survival.[62]

For Frankl, this took the form of imagining intricate conversations with his wife (who he later discovered had been murdered at another camp), or of lecturing to a future crowd about the psychology of Auschwitz. Which is of course precisely what he did for the rest of his life. *Man's Search for Meaning*, with its conclusion that "Man can preserve a vestige of spiritual freedom, of independence of mind, even in such terrible conditions of psychic and physical stress," became a massive post-war bestseller.[63] Translated into more than two dozen languages, selling over 10 millions copies, and frequently chosen by book clubs and college psychology, philosophy, and religion courses, *Man's Search for Meaning* occupied a place in the cultural zeitgeist of the mid-century. From Frankl and his followers' stead came whole university and hospital departments geared around both humanistic psychology and logotherapy, for though he was a physician, his form of psychoanalysis often seemed to bear more in common with a form of secularized religion than it did science.

Man's Search for Meaning is structured in two inextricably linked parts, the first constituting Frankl's Holocaust testimony (bearing similarity to classic works by figures like Ellie Wiesel and Primo Levi), and then in the second part, he elaborates on the principles of logotherapy, succinctly arguing that the meaning of life is found "by experiencing something—such as goodness, truth and beauty— by experiencing nature and culture or ... by experiencing another human being in his very uniqueness—by loving him," not simply in spite of apocalyptic situations *but because of them*, because the urgency of now calls for love all the more.[64]

Man's Search for Meaning has been maligned as promoting a type of superficial, pop-existentialism; a vestige of middle-brow culture that offers platitudinous New Age panaceas for problems.[65] Such a reading isn't entirely unfair; reading Frankl seven decades later, one blanches at the sexist language or the hokey suggestion that a "Statue of Responsibility" be constructed on the West Coast.[66] However, a fuller consideration of Frankl's concept of "tragic optimism" should give more attention to the former rather than the later before the therapist is impugned as overly rosy, for when he writes, "Since Auschwitz we know what man is capable of. And since Hiroshima we know what is at stake," it's hard to accuse him of being a Pollyanna.[67]

Some critics have accused Frankl of victim blaming, with scholar Lawrence Langer writing that *Man's Search for Meaning* is "almost sinister."[68] According to Langer, Frankl reduced survival to simply an issue of a positive outlook, so that consequently *Man's Search for Meaning* does a profound disservice to the millions who perished.

A critique such as this has some merits to it, and yet Frankl's actual implications are something different. His book evidences no moralizing against those who'd lost a sense of meaning; Frankl's study doesn't advocate logotherapy as an ethical act but as a strategic one.

When identifying sources of meaninglessness, it would be a mistake to find its origin within the individual who suffers under its burden. Frankl's fellow prisoners were not responsible for being in Auschwitz, just as somebody born into a cycle of poverty isn't at fault for their status, or how none of us (unless you happen to be an oil executive) is individually the cause of our collapsing ecosystem. Furthermore, nothing in logotherapy implies tacit acceptance of the status quo, for struggle to alter political, material, social, cultural, and economic conditions is, of course, paramount. What logotherapy offers is something a bit different, a way to focus and envision meaning despite those things not being immediately in your control. Rabbi Harold Kushner glosses Frankl's argument by saying that "Forces beyond your control can take away everything you possess except one thing, your freedom to choose how you will respond to the situation."[69]

There's a venerable history to such an approach, from the Stoicism of ancient Greek and Roman philosophy, as exemplified by Epictetus' contention that "the more we value things outside our control, the less control we have," to the principles of the 12 Step Movement with its focus on the minister Reinhold Niebuhr's "Serenity Prayer," imploring the penitent to be granted the "serenity to accept that which cannot be changed, the courage to change that which can, and the wisdom to know the difference."[70] Neither are reducible to logotherapy, but all of these phenomena share certain affinities, chiefly the question of how one is able to psychologically and spiritually endure when faced with an enormity far more powerful than oneself. Far from being obsessed with some universal meaning of life, logotherapy demands that the patient orient themselves to the idea of individual meaning in the moment, to "think of ourselves as those who were being questioned by life—daily and hourly" as Frankl writes.[71] Logotherapy—asking a patient to clear an imaginative space that allows them to orient themselves toward some higher meaning—is meant to provide such a response to intolerable situations.

He writes that he "grasped the meaning of the greatest secret that human poetry and human thought and belief have to impart: *The salvation of man is through love and in love.*"[72] Easy to be cynical about such a claim, which proves Frankl's point. In our small, petty, limited, cruel era, it seems awfully hard to come across much collective human affection, and yet our pettiness, limitation, and cruelty are in their own way a response to the looming apocalypse we face. "Every age has its own collective neurosis," Frankl writes, "and every age needs its own psychotherapy to cope with it."[73] If we're exhausted, fatigued, anxious, enraged, despairing, and confused at the collapse of our individual fortunes, our social networks, our communities, our industries, our democracy, our very planet, it's no wonder we've developed a certain set of collective neurosis. Yet humanistic psychology has not been in vogue for several decades; in its place, we have fashionable sociobiology and misapplied neuroscience in the form of Panglossian Steven Pinker and the guru Svengali platitudes of Jordan Peterson.

Any reduction of the human to mere brain chemistry was something that Frankl vehemently intoned against as a "personal form of nihilism."[74] That one of our most popular psychological thinkers justifies human morality through discussions of lobster serotonin would no doubt alarm Frankl.[75] What Peterson and his acolytes offer is not meaning but a vacuous neuro-sophistry. That the Anthropocene, and all of the attendant horsemen of the apocalypse that come with it, from economic insecurity to rising authoritarianism, should compel people to search for psychological answers is neither surprising nor undesirable. What logotherapy could perhaps offer is a way of approaching that issue of meaninglessness, of finding purpose when everything else is falling apart.

What this practically looks like is deceptively simple, for in orienting ourselves to meaning Frankl suggests finding purpose in genuine connection with other human beings, in the creation and appreciation of beautiful things for their own sake and not for some larger economic utility, and in believing in the radical freedom to create our own meanings separate from larger institutions and ideologies. All of this sounds so simple as to be simple-minded, and yet in late capitalism, with its increasing wealth disparity, financial insecurity resulting from the gig economy, and frayed community bonds, Frankl's suggestions can be a struggle. That's only to underscore what's valuable in logotherapy at this juncture, not that it'll save the world, or even an individual soul, but that it provides wisdom for how to find meaning in the present as the sea levels and temperature rise. Meaning is creative work, but searching for transcendence becomes even more imperative when facing the apocalypse.

In one of the most remarkable passages of *Man's Search for Meaning*, Frankl recounts how, when his work group was finally allowed a meager few hours of rest, a fellow prisoner interrupted them and "asked us to run out to the assembly grounds and see a wonderful sunset."[76] With a prose style that tends toward the clinical, albeit with a distinct sense of the sacred, Frankl here gives himself over to the transcendent, to the numinous. "Standing outside we saw sinister clouds glowing in the west and the whole sky alive with clouds of ever-changing shapes and colors, from steel blue to blood red. The desolate grey mud huts provided a sharp contrast, while the puddles on the muddy ground reflected the flowing sky." From this vision, here in a place whose very definition was in the nullification of meaning, another prisoner could remark, "How beautiful the world *could* be!"

Such is the promise of logotherapy—not to ensure that there will be more sunsets, but rather the promise to be in awe at a sunset even if it does happen to be our last one, to find wonder, meaning, beauty, and grace even in the apocalypse, even in hell. The rest is up to us.

Part Four: Writing for Preservation

Consider, Boethius. In the sixth century, he found himself imprisoned, accused of treason, in a Lombardy prison. To console himself as he awaited execution, he synthesized all of his philosophical knowledge and attempted to still his mind even as fortune's wheel turned. In his *De Consolatione Philosophiae*, he lamented, "Mad fortune sweeps along in wanton pride … Now tramples mighty kings beneath her feet."[77] He was executed in 524, supposedly with a rope around his head pulled so tightly that his eyes popped out. In this world of entropy, Boethius' task was both personal and communal, for in stoically embracing the decisions of the goddess Fortuna he admitted that death would soon come, but as he was also a refugee from a world that was dying his manuscript served as an *ars moriendi* for culture, too. And in subsequent centuries, his accomplishment was steadfastly maintained by fellow humanists, laboring in monasteries and libraries dotting Europe, making *The Consolation of Philosophy* one of the most copied texts of late antiquity, a capsule from one culture's final moments through the eclipse of the next centuries.

In not unrelated news, it was above freezing at the North Pole on December 31, 2015. We may not be so different from Boethius. It's worth thinking about him, and how he faced extinction both personal and communal, and what exactly his and our humanities are good for as we face our own civilization, possibly approaching its conclusion. A rough contemporary of Boethius noted that "in the middle of the debris of the great city, only scattered groups of wretched peoples, witnesses to past calamities, still attest to us the names of an earlier age."[78] For UCLA professor Linda Marsh, that description of the distant past sounds similar to one of the near future. In her essay "Scorched Earth, 2200 AD," she describes, "Once-teeming metropolises ... [that are now] watery ghost towns ... sparsely populated colonies of hardy survivors who eke out vampire-like subterranean existences, emerging only at night when the temperatures dip into the low-triple digits."[79] As we face a potential climate apocalypse, the question we must ask is, what are the humanities for?

Both the monasteries of the Middle Ages as well as scholars in the Islamic east preserved the classical knowledge that they could, but how would things have been different had the Romans more fully seen collapse coming? We have a benefit in being able to anticipate and plan for the possibility of our civilization's collapse, a luxury Boethius didn't exactly have. Harvard professor Naomi Oreskes and Erik Conway explain that coming "losses—social, cultural, economic, and demographic" may be "greater than any in recorded history."[80] Humanity, after all, survived the fall of Rome; it's a sunny assumption that we will make it through this time. To quote Dr. Johnson, "Nothing focuses the mind like a hanging." Well, it's time for us to focus our minds.

If science's role in all of this is to try and save the world, the humanists' is in part to preserve it. If there are future historians, they may be as befuddled with our "culture wars" as we are with the scholastic abstractions of ancient church councils. This is not to say that our "culture wars" are unimportant—or indeed that what those church councils debated was unimportant either. But perhaps it's time for a détente. These arguments will seem less significant once the West Antarctic ice sheet has collapsed into the ocean. But let us not doubt the importance of what it is that we could offer the world, as

Scranton writes, "The fate of the humanities, as we confront the end of modern civilization, is the fate of humanity itself."[81] The humanities provide a methodology for critical analysis, and also an approach to preservation. Both of these roles are crucial as we decide what material to save, and how to save it.

As we face collapse, we must initiate a "New Curating" to preserve what could be lost in the coming darkness. If everything else closes, some of us would do well to try and man the library. Think of what we've lost from the past. Unless a dutiful archeologist finds some preserved papyrus in the desert, you will never read Aristotle's second book of the *Poetics* (on comedy). Only six of the ninety plays of Aeschylus survive. Aristophanes fared a bit better, of the forty written, we have eleven. Of scripture that no one shall ever preach from, we have the *Acts of Uziah, Laments for Josiah,* or the *Story of the Prophet Iddo*.[82] Closer to our own time, and considering my subject, a particularly poignant book that none of us can ever read is the thirteenth-century travelogue *Inventio Fortunata* in which a Franciscan author describes the North Atlantic—which was cold, once. Of that most prolific author who goes by the name "Anonymous," we have even less. No doubt works of incomparable beauty and truth were spoken and penned by those on the margins—many of them women, slaves, and the conquered—and the bulk of these sit in no library.

The vast majority of our culture, western and eastern, has been lost. It has been victim to war, weather, entropy, disinterest, and decay. What we think of as the canon sometimes survived more due to the inscrutable turning of Boethius' wheel. It was humanists in the past that preserved these works, copying down manuscript to manuscript, in a thread connecting antiquity to their moment to our own day. We must be new monastics, preparing what we can to endure the interim, which we may shortly face. Scholars at places like the Long Now Foundation and Oxford University's Future of Humanity Institute are asking for us to reorient our perspective, and eco-critical scholars have been asking similar questions as well. Perhaps the humanities train people how to be more innovative thinkers in a market economy, and that might be fine justification in the short run to keep classes full, but in the "long now" the importance of the humanities takes on an obvious and profound import—that is nothing less than ensuring the preservation of our voices and thoughts unto the next generation. And we must consider that since so much of what we think of as the "canon" are works that survived because of the relative prestige of their authors, we may now have the chance to curate a more democratic list of artists, ones that reflect a diversity of human experience that was erased in the past, but whose current voices we have a responsibility to preserve for the future.

We need to ensure that scholars on the other side of the darkness are able to read Walt Whitman, Langston Hughes, or Emily Dickinson as we wish we could read the lost plays of Aristophanes. Will people be able to listen to rock and hip-hop, or watch Kubrick, Scorsese, and Kurosawa? That so much of our crucial digital culture may be impossible to preserve is the sort of central problem that a New Curating must address. In speaking of why we must curate such an ark of culture, we must remember precisely why it is that the humanities are important. Perhaps apocalypse can help us to clarify that mission in the same way that Wallace Stevens claimed, "Death is the mother of beauty."[83] At the risk of tautology, what is important about the humanities is the human; the survival of these texts is the survival of humanity. In the present day, we also must undertake this New Curating in part for our own selfish reasons—so that the future may remember us, what was important in our lives, what our experiences were. And what shall be lost, that which our monks must copy into codices for future humans to recite? In the future, there will be no summer trips down the canals of the Dutch capital, her colorful, resplendent tulip markets long since sunk; the Doge's palace and St. Mark's Square shall slide into the Adriatic, who will finally be victorious in her war of attrition against the most serene republic; and autumnal Central Park will sit under Atlantic waves, the Empire State building and World Trade Center rising up out of turbulent, warm waters.

Envision a hypothetical anthology of literature based around the seasons—the frozen landscape of an Alice Munro short story, the melancholic autumn chill of Washington Irving, the Chilean spring of a Neruda love sonnet, or even the frantic, Jersey summer of a Bruce Springsteen song. Now, as climate change becomes more extreme and unpredictable, as chaos erases those formerly independent, sovereign nations that were the seasons, consider how alien such an anthology's recorded experiences will seem to your grandchildren, and their grandchildren. That such a hypothetical anthology might seem so foreign to them is all the more reason to press the flowers of culture in a New Curating. Our grandchildren will not remember the seasons. For our and their sakes, the ark must not merely make room for Shakespeare and Goethe, but for the experiential specificity of what it was like to see the leaves change color, or the first snowfall of early winter, or the cool breeze of spring as the ice started to melt. Because it is so omnipresent, we do not appreciate the sacred power of the calendar. The twelve months are a liturgy of everyday life, still patterned, structured, and punctuated by the rhythms of temperature and the cycles of seasonal transition. We must resolve to remember what it was like when it still existed. In her beautiful "Elegy for a Country's Seasons," Zadie Smith wrote of the newly erratic weather, an increasing abolition of the seasons which we've all noticed by now. "In the end, the only thing that could create the necessary traction in our minds was the intimate loss of the things we loved."[84]

By the waters of the Atlantic, and the Pacific, and the Indian, we shall lie down and weep, for how shall we remember you Amsterdam, Venice, New York, or for that matter Mumbai, Guangzhou, or Jakarta, in this brave new world, with so few people in it? Our tongues should cleave to the roof of our mouths, and our hands should wither, for we did not save you when we could. Memory is but a veil of shadows, but it may be all that we have left, and it is the job of the humanist to preserve these songs, it is to record testimony and to bear witness for the coming wars, and genocides, and collapses. As the humanities had to face apocalypse before, so shall she have to face it again. Let us begin.

10

Letter from the Collapse—January 7, 2022 (McClean, VA)

> *The crisis consists precisely in the fact that the old is dying and the new cannot be born; in this interregnum a great variety of monsters are born.*
>
> ANTONIO GRAMSCI, *PRISON NOTEBOOKS* (1930)

In our corner of Northern Virginia, we were fortunate to never see the dead birds. Yet throughout the Mid-Atlantic—a cardinal on the pebbly beaches of Delmarva or a sparrow on the Jersey Shore, a finch like an omen in front of Independence Hall or a bluebird as a threat on the steps of the Capitol—the creatures started to die by the thousands.[1] With little sense of this new plague, experts recommended the removal of bird feeders. And so, I dutifully took down the tall model where I examined mourning doves over morning coffee and listened to woodpeckers on the birches, watched the hawks who flew above, and the sleek, elegant crows speaking in their own impenetrable tongue. *The Allegheny Front*, an environmental show on Pittsburgh's WYEP, posted a photograph of an afflicted robin found in Erie, Pennsylvania.[2] Laid out in a cardboard box decorated with spruce leaves, it looked like the otherwise pristine creature was sleeping, the only sign of its illness the thick crust on her sealed eyes. An effect not unlike the wisps of cotton that escape from underneath the lids of taxidermized birds. "The phenomenon has since spread through 10 states," writes Andy Kubis at *The Allegheny Front*, "including West Virginia, Ohio, Maryland and Delaware, and in 61 of 67 Pennsylvania counties." Observers noted neurological symptoms, birds unable to fly or crashing into the ground; the dead animals, found framed by the brittle, yellow grass of sweltering June, with the characteristic discharge from eyes and beaks.

Ornithologists proffered hypotheses, noting that the avian pandemic accompanied the cicada Brood X. Those creatures we couldn't avoid seeing, skeletal eldritch horrors bursting from the earth and their own bodies; red-eyed grotesqueries whose incessant droning permeated the humid air for weeks, who dropped from branches and through car windows like something out of a horror film. Between the dead birds and the cicadas, the summer had a Pharaonic glean, intimations of Exodus. A surreal poetry to these chthonic beings, the existential crisis of their lives spent hibernating for seventeen years, only to emerge and then die. "Happy the Cicadas live," wrote Charles Darwin in *Descent of Man, and Selection in Relation to Death*, though quoting Xenarchus.[3] Our dog took to biting them in half and pushing them between the slots of our deck's wooden planks, casting them back to hell. By the time they disappeared, without even bothering to say goodbye, I'll confess that we missed them.

But in their brittle, green bodies, there was an answer to the bird pandemic, for it seemed that people had attempted to poison the cicadas, and after ingesting their pesticide-corrupted corpses, the birds were killed instead.[4] A "sense of cosmic significance is mostly unique to the human relationship with birds," writes Borian Sax in *Avian Illuminations: A Cultural History of Birds*, though we're apparently willing to overlook that connection when it comes to using pesticides to kill insects, with our feathered friends counted as collateral damage. The same humans who undoubtedly water their lawn during a drought, or who buy the last ten chickens during the coming food shortages.[5] Trillions of cicadas emerged; to avoid them was an impossibility, but you only had to bear them for a short while, and yet people, unable to reason that there is no eliminating something of that magnitude and too impatient to wait, decided that they knew better. Is there a more perfect encapsulation of the American mindset in these dwindling days?

I'd be amazed if you couldn't sense it—the coming *end* of things. A woman sits by her grandmother in a St. Louis, Missouri, ICU, the older woman about to be intubated because Covid has destroyed her lungs, but until a day before, she insisted that the disease wasn't real. In Kenosha, Wisconsin, a young man discovers that even after murdering two men, a jury will say that homicide is justified, as long as it's against those whose politics the judge doesn't like.[6] Similar young men take note. Somebody's estranged father drives to Dallas, Texas, where he waits outside of Deeley Plaza alongside hundreds of others, expecting the emergence of JFK, Jr., who he believes is coming to crown the man who lost the last presidential election.[7] Somewhere in a Menlo Park, California, recording studio, a dead-eyed programmer with a haircut that he seems to think makes him look like Caesar Augustus stares unblinkingly into a camera and announces that his internet services will be subsumed under one meta-platform, trying to convince an exhausted, anxious, and depressed public into the piquant joys of virtual sunshine and virtual wind.[8]

At an Atlanta, Georgia, supermarket, a cashier who made minimum wage politely asks a customer to wear a mask per the store's policy; he leaves and returns with a gun, shooting her. She later dies.[9] The rural mail carrier who has driven down the winding, unnamed roads of a northwestern Oregon hamlet for over three decades notes to herself how the explosion of annoying insects on her windshield seemed entirely absent this summer. A trucker who lives in Ohio blows his airline break, and when trying to get a replacement, finds that it's on backorder indefinitely. Walking across Boston Common this October, two men holding hands and heading toward the duck boats realize that they're both sweating under their matching pea coats. It's 83 degrees. On the first day of July, my family huddles in our basement; a tornado has formed in the District of Columbia and is rapidly moving across the National Mall.

Everyone's favorite Slovenian Marxist Slavoj Žižek wrote a decade ago in *Living in the End Times* that the "global capitalist system is approaching an apocalyptic zero-point," identifying four horsemen in the form of environmental collapse, biogenetics, systemic contradictions, and "explosive growth of social divisions and exclusions."[10] Not everyone claims to see the gathering storm, however, especially those who are most responsible, though if they do, they're silent about it in their New Zealand compounds.[11] Degenerated, chipper faux-optimism is a grift during our epoch of dusk; Jeff Bezos expecting us to clap when he shoots Captain Kirk into space; Elon Musk mouth-breathing about cryptocurrency and terraforming the rusty soil of Mars, as if we haven't already heated one planet too much; Peter Thiel promising us that there will be a digital heaven where all of the billionaires can download their consciousness unshackled from the material world, and we can serve alongside them as Egyptian slaves entombed with their masters, clicking on PayPal, and Amazon, and Facebook for a silicon eternity.[12]

Such promises are the opposite of hope; they're only grinning assurances of dystopia instead of apocalypse. Besides, these assurances are chimerical; ask not for whom the Antarctic ice shelf collapses, or for whom the ocean acidifies, or for whom the temperature has risen at 3 degrees Celsius, it does all these things for Bezos, Musk, and Thiel as much as you and me. Ours is the age of Covid and QAnon, supply chain breakdown and surveillance capitalism, food shortages and armed militias, climate change and bio-collapse. We're merely in a milquetoast interregnum as we wait for monsters to be born in a year, in three. If poets and prophets have traditionally been our Cassandras, then on some level, everybody knows that a rough beast is slouching toward Bethlehem right now, though despite that, one sees perilously little grace, kindness, and empathy. Even the insanity of those who believe whatever conspiracy theory happens to give them scant meaning intuit that the insects are disappearing, the waters are rising, and the absence of 700,000 lives means that something is askance.[13]

"The world sinks into ruin," wrote St. Jerome in 413, some six decades and change before the final sack of Rome that marks the Western empire's fall. "The renowned city, the capital of the Roman Empire, is swallowed up in one tremendous fire," he noted of the Visigoth Alaric's siege.[14] Hard not to imagine that some didn't realize the end was coming, shortages of pungent garum made in Mauretania, a scarcity of Cappadocian lettuce and Pontic fish. In 410, the Emperor Honorius recalled all legions from Britannia to defend the eternal city from the Visigoths who would soon traipse through its burning streets. Envision that horde, ascending the marble steps of the Senate, in furs and horned helmets, brandishing their red standard and crowding through the halls of that once august and solemn space. Can you even countenance it? The Romanized Celts requested from the emperor the return of defensive legions, and in his rescript, Honorius "wrote letters to the cities in Britain urging them to be on their [own] guard."[15]

The United States Postal Service will be late in delivering packages, because of supply chain shortages, there is no chicken available at the Stop n Shop, the power grid will be down this winter in Texas. You're on your own. As civil society crumbled, Romans turned to all varieties of superstitions and occultisms, cults, and conspiracies. As Edward Gibbon noted in *The History of the Decline and Fall of the Roman Empire*, the "zeal of fanaticism prevailed over the cold and feeble efforts of policy."[16] *Stop the steal! Lock her up! Make America GREAT again!* Living on a heating planet filled with dying animals and governed by either the inept or the insane, it's hard not to feel a bit strange going to work, buying groceries, saving your salary, as if everything were normal. "We live as though we are going to die tomorrow," wrote Jerome, "yet we build as though we are going to live always," or, as David Byrne sang, "Why stay in college? Why go to night school? … I ain't got time for that now."

Whenever comparisons are made between Rome and America, there's always somebody who denounces such language as not just histrionic but clichéd. The latter is certainly fair; ever since the founders obsessed over republican virtue, we've imagined that the Potomac is the Tiber, and we've parsed (arch-royalist) Gibbon's history for clues about our falling. Copies of Plutarch and Livy were brought to the Continental Congress, and the most popular colonial American play was a turgid script by Joseph Addison about Cato (it would be performed at Valley Forge); the young Republic declared itself to be a "*Novus ordo seclorum*," a "New Order of the Ages," in conspicuous Latin borrowed from Virgil's *Aeneid*, while the Federalist

Papers were written under pennames like Caesar, Brutus, and Publius and John Adams attributed his worldview to Cicero.[17]

Roman symbolism was replete, as in the *fasces* that would adorn the *Senate* located on *Capitol Hill*. When George Washington deigned not to hold a third term, he was compared to the noble dictator Cincinnatus, who dropped his sword for a plow, which was enough virtue that by 1840, four decades after the first president's death, the sculptor Horatio Greenough rendered the general as a muscular Jupiter in a toga. By the final year of the Civil War, the first president was depicted underneath the Capitol dome as a purple-robed Roman god in *The Apotheosis of Washington*. The Lincoln Memorial, the Supreme Court, the Capitol, all of it neoclassical ridiculousness. Gore Vidal recalled in *United States Essays: 1952–1992* that his grandfather, Senator Thomas Gore of Oklahoma, remarked to Franklin Delano Roosevelt about the bloated buildings of Washington, "At least they will make wonderful ruins."[18] Vidal, that classical patrician, wrote that "Empires are dangerous possessions ... Since I recall pre-imperial Washington, I am a bit of an old Republican in the Ciceronian mode, given to decrying the corruption of the simpler, saner city of my youth." Hardly a postbellum pose, for critics have feared that the Republic would slide into an Empire before the Constitution's ink was dry.

Naturally, there is also fear of collapse, and long has there been foreboding about the decline and fall of the American Empire. On the top floor of the austere New-York Historical Society, there is a pentad of paintings by the unjustly forgotten landscape artist Thomas Cole, a series known as "The Course of Empire."[19] Rendered between 1833 and 1836, Cole was disturbed by both the vulgarity of Jacksonian Democracy and the brutality of Manifest Destiny. A member of the Hudson Valley School who reveled in the sheer grandiosity of the nation's natural spaces, Cole imagines in "The Course of Empire" a fantastical country from its primitive state of nature, through an idealized agrarian state, into a decadent imperium, an apocalyptic collapse, and finally desolation. Overlooking each painting is the same mountain peak, roughly the shape of Gibraltar's rock, the one consistency as Cole's civilization follows the course of its evolution, a reminder that nature was here before, and despite how we may degrade it, will still be here afterward.

The penultimate landscape, entitled simply *Destruction*, presents the denouement of this fantastic city, a skyline of columned, porticoed, and domed classical buildings in flames, bellowing smoke partially obscuring that reliable mountain; vandals flooding the streets, murdering and raping the city's citizens, pushing them into the mighty river that bisects it. A triumphant monumental statue is now decapitated. With its wide marble buildings and its memorials, Cole's city resembles nothing so much as Washington, D.C., though when he lived, the capital was more provincial backwater than the neoclassical stage set it would become. Cole made a note that "the decline of nations is generally more rapid than their rise," concluding that "Description of this picture is perhaps needless; carnage and destruction are its elements."

Enthusiasm for such parallels, along with attendant breathless warnings (including the ones that I'm making) has hardly abated. In just the past decade, there have been articles entitled "8 striking parallels between the U.S. and the Roman Empire" by Steven Strauss in 2012 at *Salon*, Pascal Emmanuel-Gobry's "America now looks like Rome before the fall of the Republic" from 2016 in *The Week*, Tim Elliot's 2020 piece at *Politico* entitled "America is Eerily Retracing Rome's Steps to a Fall. Will It Turn Around Before It's Too Late?," *Vox*'s essay from that same year, "What America Can Learn from the Fall of the Roman Republic" by Sean Illing, and Cullen Murphy's succinct "No, Really, are we Rome?" from *The Atlantic* of this year.[20]

Just to dissuade those who parse such things, Tom Holland wrote "America Is Not Rome. It Just Thinks It Is" for *The New York Review of Books* in 2019.[21] With an article that reprints Cole's painting underneath the headline, a pull-quote reads, "There is nothing written into the DNA of a superpower that says that it must inevitably decline and fall." Well, with all due respect, the second law of thermodynamics mandates that everything has to fall apart, but Holland's point is taken in a more immediate sense; comparisons of America to Rome tell us little about the latter and everything about the former. But for those who see the comparison as tortured beyond all reasonableness, the truth can be bluntly stated as follows—our current problems aren't like the fall of Rome because they're *far, far worse*. Were we only facing the collapse of the U.S. government, or authoritarianism, or even civil war, because the rising average temperature per year, the pH of the oceans, and the biodome's decreasing diversity are things unheard of on the earth since the Permian-Triassic extinction of over 250 million years ago, when 70 percent of life on land and almost 95 percent in the seas perished.[22]

"It is worse, much worse, than you think," writes Wallace-Wells in his book adaptation of his essay, also titled *The Uninhabitable Earth: Life After Warming*.[23] Wallace-Wells describes the five previous mass extinctions which shaped evolution, explaining that four of these "involved climate change produced by greenhouse gas."[24] Before the Permian-Triassic extinction, the land was occupied by the fin-reptile Dimetrodon and the hog-shaped Lystrosaurus, the abundant atmospheric oxygen supported massive dragonflies and centipedes, and the oceans were plentiful with mollusks and trilobites. For some still-unexplained reason, the amount of carbon dioxide rapidly increased, which in turn triggered the release of methane, so that this feedback loop "ended with all but a sliver of life on Earth dead," as Wallace-Wells writes. "We are currently adding carbon to the atmosphere at a considerably faster rate; by most estimates, at least ten times faster," he explains.

If we didn't know what caused that warming 250 million years ago, we know what's doing it now—us. Should the worst-case scenario of the United Nations Intergovernmental Report on Climate Change come to pass, then in the coming century the exponential increase in warming will result in an ice-free arctic; obliteration of the coastal cities where two-thirds of humans live (no more Jakarta and Bangkok, San Francisco and Miami); the mass destruction of farm land; continual massive wildfires for which we will look back fondly on the summer of 2021; never-ending hurricanes and tropical storms, heat waves, droughts, desertification, new pandemics; and at worse the acidification of the ocean and the resultant perishing of most things that live beneath the waves.[25] Short of a social or political revolution to reorient the world away from the cannibalistic capitalism that has brought us to this moment, we'll read Gibbon as halcyon (assuming anyone is around to read).

This summer, I threw a little digital life buoy out into the whirlpool of Twitter, another one of those horsemen of dystopia, and asked others what it felt like to be living during what could be the apocalypse. Mostly, I discovered that my anxiety is common, but one gentleman reminded me that there were Medieval millenarians and Great Awakening Millerites awaiting their messiahs who never came, and that they were all mistaken. That is, if you'll forgive me, exceedingly stupid. There have been times when I was sure that I was going to die—the shaky prop plane flying low to the ground between Philly and the Lehigh Valley and the erratic driver going twenty miles over the speed limit who almost side-swiped me on a stretch of I-95 in Massachusetts—but just because I survived shouldn't lead me to conclude that I'm immortal. Armageddon isn't any different. My critic, though, seems to be in the minority—most people, at least of my generation, have that sense of foreboding, picking up whatever cries are coming from the earth that the summers feel hotter, the animals scarcer, the sky sometimes glazed an ungodly glow from the redness of western fires.

"The piers are pummeled by the waves; / In a lonely field the fain / Lashes an abandoned train," wrote W.H. Auden in his 1953 poem "The Fall of Rome," perhaps about his own justified fears regarding nuclear conflagration.[26] I imagine the poet placing his wrinkled, droopy, hang-dog face to the ground and picking up on those frequencies that are today a cacophony, the "Private rites of magic" that now mark the fascists of one of our only two parties, how "an unimportant clerk / Writes I DO NOT LIKE MY WORK" reminding me of the striking heroes who are leaving the degrading and barely remunerated labor of late capitalism, how the "Herds of reindeer move across / Miles and miles of golden moss" in a warm arctic, and my beloved "Little birds with scarlet legs … Eye each flu-infected city."

From the Greek, "apocalypse" means to "uncover" hidden knowledge, so for those of us anticipating what the future holds, it's been the apocalypse for a while. What are you to do with this knowledge? Our politics operate on inertia and project onto individuals a responsibility which was always vested in the powerful themselves. Perhaps you should ditch your car, turn off your air conditioning, recycle, give up meat, and begin composting, but do that because those things are good for your soul, not because you're under any illusions that preventing the apocalypse is a consumer choice. Be neither a defeatist nor certainly an accelerationist, however, because we do have to put our shoulder to the wheel in avoiding the boiling of the oceans and the burning of the air. "To hope is to give yourself to the future," writes Rebecca Solnit in *Hope in the Dark*, "and that commitment to the future is what makes the present inhabitable."[27] Waiting for transformation like it's the messiah isn't preferable to collectively willing that transformation, but I know not what that will look like because I'm not a professional revolutionary.

The signs that are appearing in the windows of McDonald's and Subway, Starbucks and Chipotle, from workers tired of being mistreated and underpaid, represent the largest labor rebellion in a generation, the totally organic Great Resignation spoken of everywhere and reported on nowhere—it gives me hope.[28] It gives me hope because that dark faith, the capitalism that has spoiled the planet, isn't inviolate; a confirmation of Ursula K. LeGuin's promise about how all systems are finite in time, including capitalism. A corollary is the welcome mocking of fools like Bezos, Musk, and Thiel. Just the widespread awareness of our situation is promising, not because I valorize despair but maybe if there are a billion little apocalypses, it will somehow stave off the big Apocalypse. The whole of the law is to treat others as you would wish to be treated and don't cross a picket line; the rest is all theory. Now, go, and study.

Finally, I'm only a writer, and the most recondite type, an essayist. Could there be any role for something so insular at the end of the world? In *The Guardian*, novelist Ben Okri recommends "creative existentialism," which he claims is the "creativity at the end of time."[29] He argues that every line we enjamb, every phrase we turn, every narrative we further "should be directed to the immediate end of drawing attention to the dire position we are in as a species." I understand climate change as doing something similar to what Dr. Johnson said the hangman's noose did to focus the mind. It's not words that I'm worried about wasting, but experiences. What's needed is an aesthetic imperative that we somehow live in each moment as if it's eternal and also as if it's our last. Our ethical imperative is similar: to do everything as if it might save the world, even if it's unlikely that it will. Tending one's own garden need not be selfish, though if everyone does so, well, that's something then, right?

I'm counting the liturgy of small blessings, noting the cold breeze on a December morning, the crunch of brown and red and orange leaves under foot, the sound of rain hitting my office window, the laughter of my son, and the chirping of those birds at the feeder who delight him. I've no strategy except for love. "The world begins at a kitchen table," writes Poet Laureate Joy Harjo in "Perhaps the World Ends Here."[30] She reflects that "No matter what, we must eat to live." Harjo enumerates all of the quiet domestic beauties of life, how the "gifts of earth are brought and prepared" here, and "children are given instructions on what it means to be human" while sitting at this table, where "we sing with joy, with sorrow. We pray of suffering and / remorse. We give thanks. / Perhaps the world will end at the kitchen table, while we are laughing and / crying, eating of the last sweet bite." That, finally, is the only ethic I know of, as the oceans flood and the fires burn, which is to be aware of our existence at the kitchen table. When the cicadas come back in seventeen years, I wonder what the world will be like for them? I hope that there will be bird song.

Notes

Introduction

1. E. Ann Kaplan, *Climate Trauma: Foreseeing the Future in Dystopian Film and Fiction* (New Brunswick, NJ: Rutgers University Press, 2015), 16.

2. "Half Life (No Celebration)," by Win Butler, produced by Win Butler, Regine Chassagne, Richard Reed Parry, Jeremy Gara, and Markus Dravs, Sony CG, released August 2, 2010.

3. "Welcome to the World of the Polycrisis," *Financial Times*, n.d., https://www.ft.com/content/498398e7-11b1494b-9cd3-6d669dc3de33.

4. Paul Krugman, *The Great Unravelling: Losing Our Way in the New Century* (New York: W.W. Norton, 2004).

5. Timothy D. Snyder, *The Road to Unfreedom: Russia, Europe, America* (New York: Penguin Random House, 2018), 10.

6. Sarah Repucci and Amy Slipowitz, "Democracy under Siege," *Freedom House*, Freedom in the World 2021: Democracy under Siege | Freedom House.

7. Eliezer Yudkowsky, interview with Andrea Miotti, *Bankless*, podcast transcript, February 23, 2023.

8. Simon Willcock, Gregory S. Cooper, John Addy and John A. Dearing, "Earlier Collapse of Anthropocene Ecosystems Driven by Multiple Faster and Noisier Drivers," *Nature Sustainability*, Vol. 6 (2023).

9. C.J.A. Bradshaw, "Underestimating the Challenges of Avoiding a Ghastly Future," *Frontiers in Conservation Science* (2021).

10. Yuangeng Huang, et al., "The Stability and Collapse of Marine Ecosystems during the Permian-Triassic Extinction Event," *Current Biology* (2023).

11 Kumar P. Tripathy, Sourav Mukherjee, Ashok K. Mishra and A. Park Williams, "Climate Change Will Accelerate the High-End Risk of Compound Drought and Heatwave Events," *Publication of the National Academy of Sciences* (2023).

12 David Wallace-Wells, *The Uninhabitable Earth: Life after Warming* (New York: Tim Duggan Books, 2019), 12.

13 Gaya Herrington, "Update to Limits to Growth: Comparing the World3 Model with Empirical Data," *Journal of Industrial Ecology* (2020).

14 Andrew Milner and J.R. Burgman, *Science Fiction and Climate Change: A Sociological Approach* (Liverpool: Liverpool University Press, 2020), 2.

15 Alexei Yurchak, *Everything Was Forever, until It Was No More: The Last Soviet Generation* (Princeton, NJ: Princeton University Press, 2006), 1.

16 Marc Fisher, *Capitalist Realism: Is There No Alternative?* (London: Zer0 Books, 2009) and Frederic Jameson, "Future City," *New Left Review* (2003).

17 Ibid. 21.

18 Horace, *The Odes of Horace*, trans. David Ferry (New York: Farrar, Strauss, and Giroux, 1998), x.

19 Ben Ware, "Nothing but the End to Come? Extinction Fragments," *e-flux* (2020).

20 John Green, *The Anthropocene Reviewed* (New York: Penguin, 2021), 7.

21 Amitav Ghosh, *The Great Derangement: Climate Change and the Unthinkable* (Chicago, IL: The University of Chicago Press, 2017), 188.

22 Tasha Haines, *Redemptive Hybridism in Post-Postmodern Writing* (New York: Bloomsbury, 2023), 5.

23 Phillip Lewis, *The Public Humanities Turn: The University as an Instrument of Cultural Transformation* (Baltimore, MD: Johns Hopkins University Press, 2024), 98.

Chapter 1

1 John Kelly, *The Great Mortality: An Intimate History of the Black Death* (New York: Harper Perennial, 2006), 11.

2 Ibid. xv.

3   Sheila Barker, *The Making of a Plague Saint*, ch. 4 in *Piety and Plague: From Byzantium to the Baroque*, ed. Franco Mormando and Thomas Worcester (Truman State University, 2007).

4   Martha Anne Wood Wolff, *The Master of the Playing Cards: An Early Engraver and His Relationship to Traditional Media*, 1979, Dissertation, Yale; UMI (ProQuest), Dissertation Services, 2002.

5   Roy Porter, *Flesh in the Age of Reason: The Modern Foundations of Body and Soul* (New York: W.W. Norton, 2005), 212.

6   John Hatcher, *The Black Death: A Personal History* (New York: De Cappo Press, 2009), 173.

7   Pia Melin, *Fåfängans förgänglighet: allegorin som livs- och lärospegel hos Albertus Pictor* (Stockholm: Stockholmia, 2006), 106.

8   Giovanni Boccaccio, *The Decameron*, trans. G.H. McWilliam (New York: Penguin, 2003).

9   Ibid. 14.

10 Albert Camus, *The Plague*, trans. Robin Buss (New York: Penguin, 2001).

11 Kate Rigby, *Dancing with Disaster: Environmental Histories, Narratives, and Ethics for Perilous Times* (Charlottesville, VA: University of Virginia Press, 2015).

12 Emily St. John Mandel, *Station 11* (New York: Vintage, 2015), 178.

13 Ibid.

14 Ibid. 132.

15 Jack London, *The Scarlet Plague* (Orinda, CA: SeaWolf Press, 2018), 22.

16 Mary Shelley, *The Last Man* (Oxford: Oxford University Press, 2008), 469.

17 Ibid. 470.

18 Tony Kushner, *Angels in America: A Gay Fantasia on National Themes: Revised and Complete Edition* (New York: Theatre Communications Group, 2013).

19 Ibid. 96.

20 Ibid. 290.

21 Randy Shilts, *And the Band Played On: Politics, People and the AIDS Epidemic* (New York: St. Martin's Press, 1987).

22 Ibid. xxi.

23 Stephen King, *The Stand: Complete and Uncut Edition* (New York: Anchor, 2012).

24 Ibid. 1155.

25 Susan Sontag, *Illness as Metaphor and AIDS and Its Metaphors* (New York: Picador, 2001), 150.

26 Max Brooks, *World War Z: An Oral History of the Zombie War* (New York: Three Rivers Press, 2007), 21.

27 Ibid. 3.

28 Hans Holbein, *Danse Macabre: The Dance of Death* (Montreal: Scriptoria, 2021).

Chapter 2

1 Andrew Solomon, *The Noonday Demon: An Atlas of Depression* (New York: Scribner, 2015).

2 Leslie Jamison, *The Recovering: Intoxication and Its Aftermath* (New York: Little, Brown, 2018).

3 Ibid. 434.

4 Ibid. 436.

5 Ibid.

6 Now This, "Italian Opera Singer Serenades Quarantined Florence amidst Coronavirus Outbreak."

Chapter 3

1 Ella Torres, "Central Park Will Be the Site of a New Hospital for Coronavirus Patients," *ABC News*, March 31, 2020.

2 Kashmira Gander, "America's COVID Deaths May Be Equivalent to a 9/11 Every Day by Christmas," *Newsweek*, December 2, 2020.

3   Bobby Allyn, "Fauci Estimates That 100,000 to 200,000 Americans Could Die from the Coronavirus," *NPR*, March 29, 2020.

4   Sharon Lerner, "2.2 Million People in the U.S. Could Die if Coronavirus Goes Unchecked," *The Intercept*, March 17, 2020.

5   Frederick W. Hawthorne, *Gettysburg: Stories of Men and Monuments* (Hanover, PA: The Association of Licensed Battlefield Guides, 1988), 54.

6   Benjamin F. Cooling, *Jubal's Early Raid on Washington 1864* (Baltimore, MD: Rockbridge Publishing, 1989), 278.

7   Michael James, "More than 1,000 in US Die in a Single Day from Coronavirus, Doubling the Worst Daily Death Toll of the Flu," *USA TODAY*, April 1, 2020.

8   Allan Sloan, "The CARES Act Sent You a $1,200 Check but Gave Millionaires and Billionaires Far More," *ProPublica*, June 9, 2020.

9   "National Capital Columns," *U.S. National Arboretum*.

10 Zachary B. Wolf, "Dollars vs. Deaths Is the Sickening Choice Created by Coronavirus," *CNN Politics*, March 23, 2020.

11 Kitanya Harrison, "The Economy of Moloch: Human Sacrifice Demanded to Appease the Markets," *Medium*, March 25, 2020.

12 Eavan Boland, *New Collected Poems* (New York: W.W. Norton, 2009).

13 Peter Manseau and Jeff Sharlet, *Killing the Buddha: A Heretic's Bible* (New York: Free Press, 2004), 28.

Chapter 4

1   Katsuichi Honda, [Main text from *Nankin e no Michi* (*The Road to Nanjing*), 1987.] *The Nanjing Massacre: A Japanese Journalist Confronts Japan's National Shame*, ed. Frank Gibney (Washington DC: M. E. Sharp, 1999).

2   Iris Chang, *The Rape of Nanking: The Forgotten Holocaust of World War II* (New York: Basic, 2012), 99.

3   Robert O. Wilson, "Background to the Crisis," *Center for Holocaust and Genocide Education, University of Northern Iowa*, December 10, 2024, https://chge.uni.edu/robert-wilson.

4   Zhang Sheng, *The Rape of Nanking: A Historical Study* (Berlin: Walter de Gruyter, 2021).

5   David Gergen, "Iris Chang and the Forgotten Holocaust," *PBS News Hour*, December 10, 2024, https://www.pbs.org/newshour/show/iris-chang-and-the-forgotten-holocaust.

6   Ibid. 100.

7   Ibid. 16.

8   Consult Anne Applebaum, *Red Famine: Stalin's War on Ukraine* (New York: Basic, 2017). The Stalin quote first appears in a *Washington Post* article of January 20, 1947.

9   "Meeting with 90-Year-Old Holodomor Witness Mykola Onyshchenko," *Holodomor Museum*, December 10, 2024, https://holodomormuseum.org.ua/en/news-museji/meeting-with-90-year-old-holodomor-witness-mykola-onyshchenko/.

10 Example quoted from, alongside other accounts, from "Survivor Testimonies, Memoirs, Diaries, and Letters," *The Holodomor Research and Education Consortium*.

11 Chris Hedges, *War Is a Force That Gives Us Meaning* (New York: Anchor, 2003).

12 Timothy Snyder, *Bloodlands: Europe between Hitler and Stalin* (New York: Basic, 2016).

13 Carl von Clausewitz, *On War*, trans. J.J. Graham (New York: Penguin, 1982), 10.

14 William Tecumseh Sherman, Speech to the Michigan Military Academy, June 19, 1879.

15 Erich Maria Remarque, *All Quiet on the Western Front*, trans. A.W. Wheen (New York: Ballantine, 1987), frontmatter.

16 Martin Booth, *Hiroshima Joe* (New York: Picador, 2003), frontmatter.

17 John Horne Burns, *The Gallery* (New York: New York Review of Books Classics, 2004), 3.

18 Sebastian Faulks, *The Vintage Book of War Fiction* (New York: Vintage, 2002), xiii.

19 Virgil, *The Aeneid*, trans. Robert Fagles (New York: Penguin, 2008), 1.

20 Homer, *The Illiad*, trans. Stanley Lombardo (New York: Hacket, 1997), 1.

21 Bryan Doerries, *The Theater of War: What Ancient Tragedies Can Teach Us Today* (New York: Knopf Doubleday, 2016), 7.

22 Elizabeth D. Samet, *Soldier's Heart: Reading Literature through Peace and War at West Point* (New York: Farrar, Strauss and Giroux, 2004), 36.

23 Alfred Lord Tennyson, *Selected Poems* (New York: Penguin, 2008), 215.

24 Ibid. 216.

25 Walt Whitman, *The Complete Poems* (New York: Penguin, 2005), 333.

26 Remarque, 50.

27 George Walter, *The Penguin Book of First World War Poetry* (New York: Penguin).

28 Ibid.

29 Paul Fussell, *The Great War and Modern Memory* (Oxford: Oxford University Press, 2013), 268.

30 Guy Cuthbertson, *Wildred Owen* (New Haven, CT: Yale University Press, 2014), 293.

31 Lorrie Goldensohn, *American War Poetry* (New York: Columbia University Press, 2006).

32 Ibid. xxiii.

33 Ibid. 161.

34 Ibid. 225.

35 Ibid. 275.

36 Ibid. 321.

37 Ibid. 366.

38 Anthony Swofford, *Jarhead: A Marine's Chronicle of the Gulf War and Other Battles* (New York: Scribner, 2003), 7.

39 W.H. Auden, *Collected Poems of Auden* (New York: Vintage, 1991), 183.

40 *World History Encyclopedia*, "Thutmose III's Battle of Megiddo Inscription," https://www.worldhistory.org/article/1102/thutmose-iiis-battle-of-megiddo-inscription/.

Chapter 5

1. Abraham Lincoln, *The Lyceum Address* (Springfield, IL, January 27, 1838).
2. For the former I specifically had in mind Black Lives Matter and the #MeToo Movement.
3. Jonathan Levinson, Conrad Wilson, James Doubek and Suzanne Nuyen, "Federal Offices Use Unmarked Vehicles to Grab People in Portland, DHS Confirms," *NPR*, July 17, 2020.
4. Teo Armus, "Kyle Rittenhouse, Charged with Killing 2 in Kenosha, Was Fixated on Supporting Police," *The Seattle Times*, August 27, 2020.
5. Gildas, *On the Ruin and Conquest of Britain*, Project Gutenberg.
6. From "The Ruin," in the Exeter Book, composed sometime between the eighth and tenth-centuries.
7. Caroline Mimbs Nyce, "QAnon Is a New American Religion," *The Atlantic*, May 14, 2020.
8. Constantin Cavafy, *The Collected Works of C.P. Cavafy* (Princeton, NJ: Princeton University Press, 1975), 18.
9. Fintan O'Toole, "Donald Trump Had Destroyed the Country He Promised to Make Great Again," *The Irish Times*, April 25, 2020.
10. Benjamin Mueller and Eleanor Lutz, "U.S. Has Far Higher Covid Death Rate than Other Wealthy Countries," *The New York Times*, February 1, 2022.
11. D.H. Lawrence, *Studies in Classic American Literature* (New York: Thomas Selzer, 1928), 92.
12. The first is a character from Sinclair Lewis' 1927 novel *Elmer Gantry* while the later is from that same author's 1935 cautionary tale of American fascism *It Can't Happen Here*.
13. Nora Neus, *24 Hours in Charlottesville: An Oral History of the Stand against White Supremacy* (Boston, MA: Beacon Press, 2023), 11.
14. John Winthrop, *A Model of Christian Charity*, 1630; Abraham Lincoln, *The Gettysburg Address* (Gettysburg, PA, November 19, 1863); Barack Obama, *Speech at the Democratic National Convention* (Boston, MA, July 27, 2004).

15 Greil Marcus, *The Shape of Things to Come: Prophecy and the American Voice* (New York: Faber and Faber, 2006), 11.

16 Felipe Fernández-Armesto, *Amerigo: The Man Who Gave His Name to America* (New York: Random House, 2007), 185.

17 Stephen Vincent Benet, "The Devil and Daniel Webster," *The Saturday Evening Post*, October 24, 1936.

18 Leonard Cohen, "The Future," *The Future*, produced by Columbia, November 24, 1992.

19 Note the allusion, ironically, to William F. Buckley.

20 Michael Laxer, "To the Veterans of the Abraham Lincoln Brigade," *The Left Chapter*.

Chapter 6

1 Joshua Mann, "Ohio Troops Halt Morgan's Raid at Battle of Buffington Island," *The Ohio Adjutant General's Office*.

2 Dennis K. Wilson, *Justice under Pressure: The Saint Albans Raid and Its Aftermath* (Lanham, MD: University Press of America, 2007), 20.

3 Allen C. Guelzo, *Gettysburg: The Last Invasion* (New York: Alfred A. Knopf, 2013).

4 Ibid. 73.

5 John Bonner, "The Murder of Colonel Ellsworth," *Harper's Weekly*, June 8, 1861.

6 Abraham Lincoln, "To Thomas Swann and Others," *Collected Works of Abraham Lincoln, Volume 7* (New Brunswick, NJ: Rutgers University Press, 1953), 438.

7 Steven Bernstein, *The Confederacy's Last Northern Offensive: Jubal Early, the Army of the Valley and the Raid on Washington* (Jefferson, NC: McFarland, 2011).

8 Adam Goodheart, "The Happiest Man in the South," *The New York Times*, December 16, 2010.

9   Elliot C. McLaughlin, "Before January 6, Insurgents Waving Confederate Flags Hadn't Been within 6 Miles of the U.S. Capitol," *CNN*, January 7, 2021.

10   Charles Sumner, "Freedom National, Slavery Sectional," Washington, DC, July 27, 1852.

11   John C. Calhoun, "Speech on the Reception of Abolition Petitions," Washington, DC, February 26, 1837.

12   Katelyn Polantz, "January 6 Rioter 'QAnon Shaman' to Get His Headdress and Spear Back, Judge Rules," *CNN*, August 5, 2024; and Kevin Costner, *The Postman*, Tig Productions, 1997, 177 minutes.

13   "Capitol Riot: What Happened to These Rioters?" *BBC*, June 9, 2022.

14   The Hughes Brothers, *The Book of Eli*, Alcon Entertainment, 2010, 118 minutes.

15   Scott MacFarlane, "Newly Obtained Video Shows Movement of Group Suspected of Constructing Jan. 6 Gallows Hours before Capitol Siege," *ABC News*, March 18, 2024.

16   Margaret Atwood, *The Handmaid's Tale* (Toronto: McClelland Stewart Houghton Mifflin Harcourt, 1985), 175.

17   Roland Emerich, *2012*, Columbia Pictures, 2009, 158 minutes.

18   Antoine Fuqua, *Olympus Has Fallen*, Millennium Films, 2013, 119 minutes. Julien Williams, "DC's Biggest Landmarks, Ranked by How Frequently They're Destroyed in Hollywood Movies," *Thrillist*, September 1, 2016.

19   Roland Emerich, *Independence Day*, 20th Century Fox, 1996, 145 minutes.

20   Maria Flood and Michael C. Frank, "How 9/11 Changed Cinema," *The Conversation*, September 10, 2021.

21   Guy Debord, *The Society of the Spectacle* (New York: Black and Red, 1967), 16.

22   Timothy Denevi, "QAnon Takes the Capitol: Culmination or Beginning?" *Literary Hub*, January 7, 2021.

23   David S. Cecelski and Timothy B. Tyson, eds., *Democracy Betrayed: The Wilmington Race Riot of 1898 and Its Legacy* (UNC Press Books, 2000).

24 Sean Wilentz, "Who's Buried in the History Books?" *The New York Times*, May 24, 2011.

25 Kynala Phillips, "How HBO's 'Watchmen' Brought the 1921 Tulsa Race Massacre to Life," *The Wall Street Journal*, June 30, 2020.

26 "Results of Lawsuits Regarding the 2020 Election," *Campaign Legal Center*.

27 "How Groups Voted in 2020," *Roper Center for Public Opinions Research*. Trump Won 58% of the White Vote in 2020.

28 Leslie Fiedler, *Love and Death in the American Novel* (Funks Grove, IL: Dalkey Archive Press, 1997), 29.

Chapter 7

1 John F. Garst, *John Henry and His People: The Historical Origin and Lore of America's Great Folk Ballad* (Jefferson, NC: McFarland, 2022).

2 Scott Reynolds Nelson, *Steel Drivin' Man: John Henry, the Untold Story of an American Legend* (Oxford: Oxford University Press, 2008), 91.

3 Ibid. 111.

4 Adrienne Mayor, *Gods and Robots: Myths, Machines, and Ancient Dreams of Technology* (Princeton, NJ: Princeton University Press, 2018), 213.

5 Paul L. Dawson, *The Battle against the Luddites: Unrest in the Industrial Revolution during the Napoleonic Wars* (New York: Frontline Books, 2023).

6 Monty Newborn, *Kasparov versus Deep Blue: Computer Chess Comes of Age* (New York: Springer, 1996).

7 Personal correspondence, January 2023.

8 Stephen Marche, "The Computers Are Getting Better at Writing," *The New Yorker*, April 30, 2021.

9 Marche, "The College Essay Is Dead," *The Atlantic*, December 6, 2022.

10 Matteo Wong, "Artists Are Losing the War against AI," *The Atlantic*, October 2, 2023.

11 Mike Sharples and Rafael Perez Y Perez, *Story Machines: How Computers Have Become Creative Writers* (London: Routledge, 2022), xii.

12 Mayor, 197.

13 Ibid. xii.

14 Jonathan Swift, *Gulliver's Travels* (New York: Penguin, 2003), 281.

15 Jorge Luis Borges, "Ramon Llull's Thinking Machine," *Selected Non-Fictions* (New York: Penguin, 2000), 159.

16 Leslie Jameson, "The Enduring Allure of Choose Your Own Adventure Books," *The New Yorker*, September 12, 2022, and Warren F. Motte Jr., *Oulipo: A Primer of Potential Literature* (Funks Grove, IL: Dalkey Archive Press, 2015).

17 Edward Packard, *The Cave of Time* (New York: Bantam, 1982) and Raymond Queneau, *Hundred Thousand Billion Poems* (Paris: Gallimard, 1962).

18 J.D. Hall, "Popular Prosody: Spectacle and the Politics of Victorian Versification," *Nineteenth-Century Literature*, Vol. 62 (2007): 222–49.

19 Mike Sharples, "John Clark's Latin Verse Machine: 19th Century Computational Creativity," *IEEE Annals of the History of Computing*, Vol. 45, No. 1 (2023): 31–42.

20 "John Clark's Latin Verse Machine: 19th Century Computational Creativity," *Electronic Literature Knowledge Base*, https://elmcip.net/critical-writing/john-clarks-latin-verse-machine-19th-century-computational-creativity.

21 "The Eureka Machine for Composing Hexameter Verses," *Minerva Classics*, https://minervaclassics.com/eureka.htm.

22 Anna P. Judson, "Eureka! It's an Automatic Latin Poetry Machine!" *It's All Greek to Me*, https://itsallgreektoanna.wordpress.com/2016/10/07/eureka-its-an-automatic-latin-poetry-machine/.

23 Ibid. Judson.

24 Anna Green, "Arthur Blanchard's 'Thinking Machine' Was the Random Story Generator of 1916," *Mental Floss*, December 7, 2015.

25 Noah Wardrip-Fruin, "Christopher Strachey: The First Digital Artist?" *Grand Text Auto* (School of Engineering, University of California Santa Cruz, August 1, 2005).

26 Homay King, *Virtual Memory: Time-Based Art and the Dream of Digitality* (Raleigh, NC: Duke University Press, 2015), 19.

27 David Leavitt, *The Man Who Knew Too Much: Alan Turing and the Invention of the Computer* (New York: W.W. Norton, 2006), 5.

28 Racter, *The Policeman's Beard Is Half-Constructed* (New York: Grand Central Publication, 1984).

29 Ines Bouteldj, "Will You Be Reading Books Written by AI in 2023?" *RTE*, December 13, 2022.

30 Karl Capek, *R.U.R.*, trans. Claudia Novack-Jones (New York: Penguin, 2004), 21.

31 Ibid.

32 Ibid. 56.

33 Ibid.

34 E.P. Thompson, *The Making of the English Working Class* (New York: Vintage, 1966).

35 Nicols Fox, *Against the Machine: The Hidden Luddite Tradition in Literature, Art, and Individual Lives* (Washington, DC: Island Press, 2002), 25.

36 David Graeber, *Bullshit Jobs: A Theory* (New York: Melville House, 2019).

37 Kirkpatrick Sale, *Rebels against the Future: Luddites and Their War on the Industrial Revolution* (New York: Basic Books, 1996), 5.

38 Kyle Dargan, *Honest Engine: Poems* (Athens, GA: University of Georgia Press, 2005), 50.

39 Stanley Fish, *Is There a Text in This Class: The Authority of Interpretive Communities* (Cambridge, MA: Harvard University Press, 1982), 14.

Chapter 8

1 Richard S.M. Hirsch, "The Works of Chidiock Tichborne," *English Literary Renaissance*, Vol. 16 No. 2 (1986): 303–18 and (1987), Vol. 17, 276–7.

2 A prime contention of Eamon Duffy in *Fires of Faith: Catholic England under Mary Tudor* (New Haven, CT: Yale University Press, 2009).

3 Emrys Jones, *The New Oxford Book of Sixteenth Century Verse* (Oxford: Oxford University Press, 2009), 393.

4   Yoel Hoffmann, *Japanese Death Poems: Written by Zen Monks and Haiku Poets on the Verge of Death* (Tokyo: Tuttle Publishing, 2018).

5   Tad Friend, "The God Pill: Silicon Valley's Quest for Eternal Life," *The New Yorker*, April 3, 2017.

6   Nathan Schneider, "An Interview with Ann Neumann, Journalist of Death," *America: The Jesuit Review*, February 16, 2016.

7   Ed Simon, "The Crucified God: A Death in Pictures," *The Marginalia Review of Books*, April 11, 2017.

8   Penry Williams, "Babington, Anthony (1561–1586)," *Oxford Dictionary of National Biography* (Oxford: Oxford University Press, 2004).

9   Karl Popper, *The Logic of Scientific Discovery* (London: Hutchingson, 1959).

10 Brendan Shea, "Karl Popper: Philosophy of Science," *Internet Encyclopedia of Philosophy*.

11 Despite the ridiculous title, the best introduction to this ideology remains Edward Regis' *Great Mambo Chicken and the Transhuman Condition: Science Slightly over the Edge* (New York: Basic Books, 1990).

12 Ingmar Bergman, *The Seventh Seal*, AB-Svensk Filmindustri, 1957, 96 minutes.

13 Ed Simon, "Ten Ways to Live Forever," *The Millions*, November 20, 2019.

14 Stephen Cave, *Immortality: The Quest to Live Forever and How It Drives Civilization* (New York: Crown, 2012), 273.

15 Julian Barnes, *Nothing to Be Frightened Of* (New York: Knopf, 2008).

16 Hans Moravec, *Mind Children: The Future of Robot and Human Intelligence* (Cambridge, MA: Harvard Belknap, 1988), 115.

17 Regis, 176.

18 Max Anderson, "Peter Thiel, N.T. Wright on Technology, Hope, and the End of Death," *Forbes*, June 24, 2015.

19 Ibid. 1.

20 John Rennie, "The Immortal Ambitions of Ray Kurzweil: A Review of *Transcendent Man*," *Scientific American*, February 11, 2011.

21. John Gray, "Dear Google, Please Solve Death: Meet the Transhumanists Who Believe That the Brain Can Outlive the Body," *The New Statesman*, April 9, 2017.

22. Michel de Montaigne, *The Complete Essays* (New York: Penguin, 1993), 89.

23. Anna Wiener, "What Is It about Peter Thiel?" *The New Yorker*, October 27, 2021.

24. Percy Shelley, *Collected Poems and Prose* (New York: Penguin, 2017).

25. Mary Beard, *The Roman Triumph* (Cambridge, MA: Harvard Belknap, 2007), 85–92.

26. Quoted in Friend's article.

27. Terry Gross, "Maurice Sendak: On Life, Death and Children's Lit," *All Things Considered*, NPR, December 29, 2011.

Chapter 9

1. Thomas Halliday, *Otherlands: A Journey through Earth's Extinct Worlds* (New York: Random House, 2022), 174.

2. Helen Gordon, *Notes from Deep Time: A Journey through Our Past and Future* (New York: Profile Books, 2022).

3. Martin Sheldrake, *Entangled Life: How Fungi Make Our World, Change Our Minds & Shape Our Futures* (New York: Random House, 2020), 49.

4. Elizabeth Kolbert, *The Sixth Great Extinction: An Unnatural History* (New York: Henry Holt, 2014), 80.

5. Primo Levi, *The Periodic Table* (New York: Schocken Books, 1975), 240.

6. Pitchaya Sudbanthad, "A Brief History of Breathing," *The World as We Know It: Dispatches from a Changing Climate*, ed. Amy Brady and Tajja Isen (New York: Catapult, 2022), 38.

7. Pieter Vermeulen, *Literature and the Anthropocene* (London: Routledge, 2020), 118.

8. Omar El Akkad, "Faster than We Thought," *The World as We Know It: Dispatches from a Changing Climate*, ed. Amy Brady and Tajja Isen (New York: Catapult, 2022), 88.

9   Ibid. xii.

10 Adam Trexler, *Anthropocene Fictions: The Novel in a Time of Climate Change* (Charlottesville, VA: University of Virginia Press, 2015), 6.

11 Gabriel Bellot, "Starshift," *The World as We Know It: Dispatches from a Changing Climate*, ed. Amy Brady and Tajja Isen (New York: Catapult, 2022), 15.

12 Melissa Febos, "Iowa Bestiary," *The World as We Know It: Dispatches from a Changing Climate*, ed. Amy Brady and Tajja Isen (New York: Catapult, 2022), 60.

13 Ibid. 89.

14 Caitlin O'Kane "Summer in the U.S. Could Be 8 Degrees Hotter in 2100—with Some Cities Feeling More Like the Middle East," *CBS News*, August 3, 2022.

15 Ibid. 91.

16 Ibid. 30.

17 Meera Subramanian, "Leap," *The World as We Know It: Dispatches from a Changing Climate*, ed. Amy Brady and Tajja Isen (New York: Catapult, 2022), 120.

18 Zora Neal Hurston, *Their Eyes Were Watching God* (New York: Harper Perennial, 1937), 151.

19 Roy William Scranton, *We're Doomed. Now What: Essays on War and Climate Change* (New York: Soho, 2018), 326.

20 Ursula K. Heise, *Imagining Extinction: The Cultural Meanings of Endangered Species* (Chicago, IL: University of Chicago Press, 2016), 9.

21 Ibid. 3.

22 Ibid. 77.

23 Ibid. 73.

24 Ibid. 8.

25 Ibid. 68; emphasis in original.

26 Ibid. 3.

27 Frederic Jameson. "Future City," *New Left Review* (May–June 2003).

28 Ibid. 3.
29 Ibid. 321.
30 Ibid. 6.
31 Ibid. 329.
32 Ibid. 48.
33 Mark Fisher, *Capitalist Realism: Is There No Alternative?* (London: Zer0 Books, 2009).
34 Scranton, 6.
35 Fisher, 16.
36 Scranton, 325.
37 Ibid. 320.
38 Ibid. 24.
39 Ibid. 53.
40 Hans Magnus Enzensberger, "Two Notes on the End of the World: Remarks on the Spectacle," *New Left Review* (July–August 1978.)
41 Jacques Derrida, "No Apocalypse, Not Now," *Diacritics*, Summer 1984.
42 Ed Simon, *The Dove and the Dragon: A History of the Apocalypse* (Minneapolis, MN: Fortress, 2025), 1.
43 Ibid. 77.
44 Ibid. 326.
45 Speech delivered at the 2014 National Book Awards.
46 Timothy Clark, *Ecocriticism on the Edge: The Anthropocene as a Threshold Concept* (London: Bloomsbury, 2015), xi.
47 Scranton, 8.
48 Ibid. 326.
49 Monika Kaup, *New Ecological Realisms: Post-Apocalyptic Fiction and Contemporary Theory* (Edinburgh: Edinburgh University Press, 2021).
50 Ibid. 148–9.
51 David Wallace-Wells, "The Uninhabitable Earth," *New York Magazine*, July 9, 2017.

52 Alexis Papazoglou, "Is It Cruel to Have Kids in the Era of Climate Change?" *The New Republic*, February 25, 2019.

53 Jonathan Franzen, "What If We Stopped Pretending?" *The New Yorker*, September 8, 2019.

54 Viktor Frankl, *Man's Search for Meaning* (Boston, MA: Beacon Press, 2006), 105.

55 Ibid. 20.

56 Henry Gee, "Humans Are Doomed to Go Extinct," *Scientific American*, November 30, 2021.

57 Haddon Klingberg, *When Life Calls Out to Us: The Love and Lifework of Viktor and Elly Frankl* (New York: Doubleday, 2001), 155.

58 Frankl, 99.

59 Ibid.

60 Ibid. 7.

61 Ibid. 74.

62 Ibid. 36.

63 Ibid. 65.

64 Ibid. 59.

65 Mattie Kahn, "How Instagram Turned a Holocaust Memoir into a Self-Help Manifesto," *Vox*, November 28, 2022.

66 Ibid. 132.

67 Ibid. 154.

68 Lawrence Langer, "The Literature of Auschwitz," *Anatomy of the Auschwitz Death Camp*, ed. Yisrael Gutman and Michael Berenbaum (Bloomington, IN: Indiana University Press, in association with the United States Holocaust Memorial Museum, 1994), 604.

69 Ibid. x.

70 Epictetus, *Discourse and Selected Writings* (New York: Penguin, 2008), 201, and Fred R. Shapiro, "Who Wrote the Serenity Prayer?" *Yale Alumni Magazine*, July/August 2008.

71 Ibid. 38.

72 Ibid. 37.

73 Ibid. 129.

74 Ibid.

75 Jordan Peterson, *12 Rules for Life: An Antidote to Chaos* (Toronto: Random House Canada, 2018), 7.

76 Ibid. 40.

77 Boethius, *The Consolations of Philosophy*, trans. Viktor Watt (New York: Penguin, 1999), 29.

78 Quoted by Maurice Lombard in "Urban Evolution in the Middle Ages" from *Internal Colonization in Medieval Europe*, ed. Felipe Fernandez-Armesto and James Muldoon (New York: Ashgate, 2008).

79 Linda Marsh, "Scorched Earth, 2200 A.D.," *Aeon*, February 10, 2015.

80 Naomi Oreskes and Eric Conway, *The Collapse of Western Civilization: A View from the Future* (New York: Columbia University Press, 2014), 32.

81 Ibid. 109.

82 All examples drawn from Stuart Kelley's *The Book of Lost Books: An Incomplete History of All the Great Books You'll Never Read* (London: Polygon, 2012).

83 Wallace Stevens, *The Collected Poems of Wallace Stevens* (New York: Vintage, 2015), 73.

84 Zadie Smith, "Elegy for a Country's Seasons," *The New York Review of Books*, April 3, 2014.

Chapter 10

1 "Cause of 2021 Songbird Mortality Event Remains Unknown," *Valley Forge Audubon Society*, 2021.

2 Andy Kubis, "Researchers Trying to Figure Out What's Causing Mysterious Bird Deaths," *The Allegheny Front*, July 9, 2021.

3 Charles Darwin, *The Descent of Man, and Selection in Relation to Sex* (London, 1871), 350.

4 Seth Kaplan, "'And I Knew Right Away': Could Mysterious Songbird Deaths in Pa. Be Connected to Cicadas?" *WHTM*, July 2, 2021.

5   Boria Sax, *Avian Illuminations: A Cultural History of Birds* (London: Reaktion Books, 2021), 10.

6   Becky Sullivan, "Kyle Rittenhouse Is Acquitted of All Charges in the Trial Over Killing 2 in Kenosha," *NPR*, November 19, 2021.

7   E.J. Dickson and Steven Monacelli, "On the Ground with QAnon Believers Who Flocked to Dallas for the Grand Return of JFK Jr.," *Rolling Stone*, November 2, 2021.

8   David Ingram, "Facebook Goes Meta: Zuckerberg Announces New Corporate Name," *NBC News*, October 21, 2021.

9   Eric Perry, "Cashier Dead, Deputy Injured after Dispute with Man over a Mask, GBI Says," *FOX5 Atlanta*, June 14, 2021.

10 Slavoj Zizek, *Living in the End Times* (New York: Verso, 2018), x.

11 Mark O'Connell, "Why Silicon Valley Billionaires Are Prepping for the Apocalypse in New Zealand," *The Guardian*, February 15, 2018.

12 Enrique Rivera, "William Shatner Experienced Profound Grief in Space. It Was the 'Overview Effect,'" *NPR*, October 23, 2022 and Ian Krietzberg, "SpaceX Chief Elon Musk Explains What He Needs to Do to Colonize Mars," *TheStreet*, November 1, 2023.

13 Julie Bosman and Lauren Leatherby, "U.S. Coronavirus Death Toll Surpasses 700,000 Despite Wide Availability of Vaccines," *The New York Times*, October 1, 2021.

14 Jerome, "Letter 128."

15 Quoted in David Wood, "On the Alleged Letters of Honorius to the Cities of Britain in 410," *La Revue Latomus*, September 2012, 818–26.

16 Edward Gibbon, *The History of the Decline and Fall of the Roman Empire* (London: Strahan & Cadell, 1776), 39.

17 As discussed by Bernard Bailyn in *The Ideological Origins of the American Revolution* (Cambridge, MA: Harvard University Press, 1967).

18 Gore Vidal, *United States Essays: 1952–1992* (New York: Broadway Books, 1993).

19 Thomas Cole, "The Course of Empire," c. 1833–36, oil on canvas, 39.5 × 63.5 inches, The New-York Historical Society.

20 Steven Strauss, "8 Striking Parallels between the U.S. and the Roman Empire," *Salon*, December 26, 2012; Pascal Emmanuel-Gobry, "America

Now Looks Like Rome before the Fall of the Republic," *The Week*, November 10, 2016; Tim Elliot', "America Is Eerily Retracing Rome's Steps to a Fall. Will It Turn around before It's Too Late?" *Politico*, November 3, 2020; Sean Illing, "What America Can Learn from the Fall of the Roman Republic," *Vox*, January 1, 2019; Cullen Murphy, "No, Really, Are We Rome?" *The Atlantic*, March 11, 2021.

21 Tom Holland, "America Is Not Rome. It Just Thinks It Is," *The New York Review of Books*, August 6, 2019.

22 "The Great Dying," NASA, January 27, 2002, https://science.nasa.gov/science-research/earth-science/the-great-dying/.

23 David Wallace-Wells, *The Uninhabitable Earth: Life after Warming* (New York: Crown, 2020), 3.

24 Ibid. 4.

25 Andrew Berkely and John Letzing, "The Worst-Case Climate-Change Scenario Could Look Like This. We Need to Avert It," *World Economic Forum*, September 23, 2020.

26 W.H. Auden, *Collected Poems of Auden* (New York: Vintage, 1991), 332.

27 Rebecca Solnit, *Hope in the Dark: Untold Histories, Wild Possibilities* (Chicago, IL: Haymarket, 2016), 4.

28 A. Serenko, "The Great Resignation: The Great Knowledge Exodus or the Onset of the Great Knowledge Revolution?" *Journal of Knowledge Management*, Vol. 27, No. 4 (2023): 1042–55.

29 Ben Okri, "Artists Must Confront the Climate Crisis—We Must Write as if These Are the Last Days," *The Guardian*, November 12, 2021.

30 Nick Ripatrazone, "Enormous Zippers Unfastening: Ten Poems for the End of the World," *The Millions*, April 8, 2016.

Bibliography

Allyn, Bobby. "Fauci Estimates That 100,000 to 200,000 Americans Could Die from the Coronavirus," *NPR*, March 29, 2020.

Anderson, Max. "Peter Thiel, N.T. Wright on Technology, Hope, and the End of Death," *Forbes*, June 24, 2015.

Applebaum, Anne. *Red Famine: Stalin's War on Ukraine*. New York: Basic, 2017.

Aragno, Tim, Nicholes Bogel-Burroughs and Katie Benner. "Minutes before El Paso Killing, Hate-Filled Manifesto Appears Online," *The New York Times*, August 3, 2019.

Armus, Teo. "Kyle Rittenhouse, Charged with Killing 2 in Kenosha, Was Fixated on Supporting Police," *The Seattle Times*, August 27, 2020.

Atwood, Margaret. *The Handmaid's Tale*. Toronto: McClelland Stewart Houghton Mifflin Harcourt, 1985.

Auden, W.H. *Collected Poems of Auden*. New York: Vintage, 1991.

Bailyn, Bernard. *The Ideological Origins of the American Revolution*. Cambridge, MA: Harvard University Press, 1967.

Barker, Sheila. *The Making of a Plague Saint*, ch. 4 in *Piety and Plague: From Byzantium to the Baroque*, ed. Franco Mormando and Thomas Worcester. Truman State University, 2007.

Barnes, Julian. *Nothing to Be Frightened Of*. New York: Knopf, 2008.

Beard, Mary. *The Roman Triumph*. Cambridge, MA: Harvard Belknap, 2007.

Bellot, Gabriel. "Starshift," *The World as We Know It: Dispatches from a Changing Climate*, ed. Amy Brady and Tajja Isen. New York: Catapult, 2022.

Benet, Stephen Vincent. "The Devil and Daniel Webster," *The Saturday Evening Post*, October 24, 1936.

Bergman, Ingmar. *The Seventh Seal*. AB-Svensk Filmindustri, 1957, 96 minutes.

Berkely, Andrew and John Letzing. "The Worst-Case Climate-Change Scenario Could Look Like This. We Need to Avert It," *World Economic Forum*, September 23, 2020.

Bernstein, Steven. *The Confederacy's Last Northern Offensive: Jubal Early, the Army of the Valley and the Raid on Washington.* Jefferson, NC: McFarland, 2011.

Boccaccio, Giovani. *The Decameron*, trans. G.H. McWilliam. New York: Penguin, 2003.

Boethius. *The Consolations of Philosophy*, trans. Viktor Watt. New York: Penguin, 1999, 29.

Boland, Eavan. *New Collected Poems.* New York: W.W. Norton, 2009.

Bonner, John. "The Murder of Colonel Ellsworth," *Harper's Weekly*, June 8, 1861.

Booth, Martin. *Hiroshima Joe.* New York: Picador, 2003.

Borges, Jorge Luis. "Ramon Llull's Thinking Machine," *Selected Non-Fictions.* New York: Penguin, 2000.

Bosman, Julie and Lauren Leatherby. "U.S. Coronavirus Death Toll Surpasses 700,000 Despite Wide Availability of Vaccines," *The New York Times*, October 1, 2021.

Boswell, James. *Life of Samuel Johnson.* London, 1791.

Bouteldj, Injes. "Will You Be Reading Books Written by AI in 2023?" *RTE*, December 13, 2022.

Bradshaw, C.J.A. "Underestimating the Challenges of Avoiding a Ghastly Future," *Frontiers in Conservation Science*, 2021.

Brooks, Max. *World War Z: An Oral History of the Zombie War.* New York: Three Rivers Press, 2007.

Burnham, Bo. *Bo Burnham: Inside.* Produced by Josh Senior, 2021, 87 minutes.

Burns, John. *The Gallery.* New York: New York Review of Books Classics, 2004.

Butler, Win. *The Suburbs.* Produced by Win Butler, Regine Chassagne, Richard Reed Parry, Jeremy.

Byrn, David. "Life during Wartime," *Fear of Music.* Produced by Brian Eno and the Talking Heads. Sire. August 3, 1979.

Calhoun, John C. "Speech on the Reception of Abolition Petitions," Washington, DC, February 26, 1837.

Camus, Albert. *The Plague*, trans. Robin Buss. New York: Penguin, 2001.

"Capitol Riot: What Happened to These Rioters?" *BBC*, June 9, 2022.

"Cause of 2021 Songbird Mortality Event Remains Unknown," *Valley Forge Audubon Society*.

Cavafy, Constantin. *The Collected Works of C.P. Cavafy.* Princeton, NJ: Princeton University Press, 1975.

Cave, Stephen. *Immortality: The Quest to Live Forever and How It Drives Civilization.* New York: Crown, 2012.

Cecelski, David S. and Timothy B. Tyson, eds. *Democracy Betrayed: The Wilmington Race Riot of 1898 and Its Legacy.* UNC Press Books, 2000.

Chang, Iris. *The Rape of Nanking: The Forgotten Holocaust of World War II*. New York: Basic, 2012.

Clark, Timothy. *Ecocriticism on the Edge: The Anthropocene as a Threshold Concept*. London: Bloomsbury, 2015.

von Clausewitz, Carl. *On War*, trans. J.J. Graham. New York: Penguin, 1982.

Cohen, Leonard. "The Future," *The Future*. Produced by Columbia, November 24, 1992.

Cole, Thomas. "The Course of Empire," c. 1833–36, oil on canvas, 39.5x63.5 inches, The New-York Historical Society.

Cooling, Benjamin F. *Jubal's Early Raid on Washington 1864*. Baltimore, MD: Rockbridge Publishing, 1989.

Costner, Kevin. *The Postman*. Tig Productions, 1997, 177 minutes.

Cuthbertson, Guy. *Wildred Owen*. New Haven, CT: Yale University Press, 2014.

Dargan, Kyle. *Honest Engine: Poems*. Athens, GA: University of Georgia Press, 2005.

Darwin, Charles. *The Descent of Man, and Selection in Relation to Sex*. London, 1871.

Dawson, Paul L. *The Battle against the Luddites: Unrest in the Industrial Revolution during the Napoleonic Wars*. New York: Frontline Books, 2023.

Debord, Guy. *The Society of the Spectacle*. New York: Black and Red, 1967.

Denevi, Timothy. "QAnon Takes the Capitol: Culmination or Beginning?" *Literary Hub*, January 7, 2021.

Derrida, Jacques. "No Apocalypse, Not Now," *Diacritics*, Summer 1984.

Dickson, E.J. and Steven Monacelli. "On the Ground with QAnon Believers Who Flocked to Dallas for the Grand Return of JFK Jr.," *Rolling Stone*, November 2, 2021.

Doerries, Bryan. *The Theater of War: What Ancient Tragedies Can Teach Us Today*. New York: Knopf Doubleday, 2016.

Duffy, Eamon. *Fires of Faith: Catholic England under Mary Tudor*. New Haven, CT: Yale University Press, 2009.

El Akkad, Omar. "Faster than We Thought," *The World as We Know It: Dispatches from a Changing Climate*, ed. Amy Brady and Tajja Isen. New York: Catapult, 2022.

Elliot, Tim. "America Is Eerily Retracing Rome's Steps to a Fall. Will It Turn around before It's Too Late?" *Politico*, November 3, 2020.

Ellison, Ralph. *The Invisible Man*. New York: Random House, 1952.

Emerich, Roland. *2012*, Columbia Pictures, 2009, 158 minutes.

Emerich, Roland. *Independence Day*. 20th Century Fox, 1996, 145 minutes.

Emmanuel-Gobry, Pascal. "America Now Looks Like Rome before the Fall of the Republic," *The Week*, November 10, 2016.

Enzensberger, Hans Magnus. "Two Notes on the End of the World: Remarks on the Spectacle," *New Left Review*, July–August 1978.

Epictetus. *Discourse and Selected Writings*. New York: Penguin, 2008.

"The Eureka Machine for Composing Hexameter Verses," *Minerva Classics*, https://minervaclassics.com/eureka.htm.

Faulks, Sebastian. *The Vintage Book of War Fiction*. New York: Vintage, 2002.

Febos, Melissa. "Iowa Bestiary," *The World as We Know It: Dispatches from a Changing Climate*, ed. Amy Brady and Tajja Isen. New York: Catapult, 2022.

Fernández-Armesto, Felipe. *Amerigo: The Man Who Gave His Name to America*. New York: Random House, 2007.

Fiedler, Leslie. *Love and Death in the American Novel*. Funks Grove, IL: Dalkey Archive Press, 1997.

Fish, Stanley. *Is There a Text in This Class: The Authority of Interpretive Communities*. Cambridge, MA: Harvard University Press, 1982.

Fisher, Marc. *Capitalist Realism: Is There No Alternative?* London: Zer0 Books, 2009.

Flood, Maria and Michael C. Frank. "How 9/11 Changed Cinema," *The Conversation*, September 10, 2021.

Fox, Nicols. *Against the Machine: The Hidden Luddite Tradition in Literature, Art, and Individual Lives*. Washington, DC: Island Press, 2002.

Frankl, Viktor. *Man's Search for Meaning*. Boston, MA: Beacon Press, 2006.

Franzen, Jonathan. "What If We Stopped Pretending?" *The New Yorker*, September 8, 2019.

Friend, Tad. "The God Pill: Silicon Valley's Quest for Eternal Life," *The New Yorker*, April 3, 2017.

Fuqua, Antoine. *Olympus Has Fallen*. Millennium Films, 2013, 119 minutes.

Fussell, Paul. *The Great War and Modern Memory*. Oxford: Oxford University Press, 2013.

Gander, Kashmira. "America's COVID Deaths May Be Equivalent to a 9/11 Every Day by Christmas," *Newsweek*, December 2, 2020.

Gara and Markus Dravs. "Sony CG (US)," Released August 2, 2010.

Garst, John F. *John Henry and His People: The Historical Origin and Lore of America's Great Folk Ballad*. Jefferson, NC: McFarland, 2022.

Gee, Henry. "Humans Are Doomed to Go Extinct," *Scientific American*, November 30, 2021.

Gergen, David. "Iris Chang and the Forgotten Holocaust," *PBS News Hour*, December 10, 2024, https://www.pbs.org/newshour/show/iris-chang-and-the-forgotten-holocaust.

Ghosh, Amitav. *The Great Derangement: Climate Change and the Unthinkable*. Chicago, IL: The University of Chicago Press, 2017.

Gibbon, Edward. *The History of the Decline and Fall of the Roman Empire*. London: Strahan & Cadell, 1776.

Gildas. *On the Ruin and Conquest of Britain*. Project Gutenberg.

Goldensohn, Lorrie. *American War Poetry*. New York: Columbia University Press, 2006.

Goodheart, Adam. "The Happiest Man in the South," *The New York Times*, December 16, 2010.

Gordon, Helen. *Notes from Deep Time: A Journey through Our Past and Future*. New York: Profile Books, 2022.

Gourevitch, Philip. *We Regret to Inform You That Tomorrow We Will Be Killed with Our Families*. New York: Picador, 2004.

Graeber, David. *Bullsh*t Jobs: A Theory*. New York: Melville House, 2019.

Gramsci, Antonio. *The Prison Notebooks*. New York: Columbia University Press, 1975.

Gray, John. "Dear Google, Please Solve Death: Meet the Transhumanists Who Believe That the Brain Can Outlive the Body," *The New Statesman*, April 9, 2017.

"The Great Dying," NASA, January 27, 2002, https://science.nasa.gov/science-research/earth-science/the-great-dying/.

Green, Anna. "Arthur Blanchard's 'Thinking Machine' Was the Random Story Generator of 1916," *Mental Floss*, December 7, 2015.

Green, John. *The Anthropocene Reviewed*. New York: Penguin, 2021.

Gross, Terry. "Maurice Sendak: On Life, Death and Children's Lit," *All Things Considered*, NPR, December 29, 2011.

Guelzo, Allen C. *Gettysburg: The Last Invasion*. New York: Alfred A. Knopf, 2013.

Haines, Tasha. *Redemptive Hybridism in Post-Postmodern Writing*. New York: Bloomsbury, 2023.

Hall, J.D. "Popular Prosody: Spectacle and the Politics of Victorian Versification," *Nineteenth-Century Literature* 62, 2007.

Halliday, Thomas. *Otherlands: A Journey through Earth's Extinct Worlds*. New York: Random House, 2022.

Harrison, Kitanya. "The Economy of Moloch: Human Sacrifice Demanded to Appease the Markets," *Medium*, March 25, 2020.

Hatcher, John. *The Black Death: A Personal History*. New York: De Cappo Press, 2009.

Hawthorne, Frederick W. *Gettysburg: Stories of Men and Monuments*. Hanover, PA: The Association of Licensed Battlefield Guides, 1988.

Hedges, Chris. *War Is a Force That Gives Us Meaning*. New York: Anchor, 2003.

Heise, Ursula K. *Imagining Extinction: The Cultural Meanings of Endangered Species*. Chicago, IL: University of Chicago Press, 2016.

Heller, Joseph. *Catch-22*. New York: Dell, 1975.

Hemon, Aleksander. *The Book of My Lives*. New York: Farrar, Strauss and Giroux, 2013.

Herrington, Gaya. "Update to Limits to Growth: Comparing the World3 Model with Empirical Data," *Journal of Industrial Ecology*, 2020.

Hirsch, Richard S.M. "The Works of Chidiock Tichborne," *English Literary Renaissance* 16(2), 1986: 303–18 and (1987) Vol. 17.

Hoffmann, Yoel. *Japanese Death Poems: Written by Zen Monks and Haiku Poets on the Verge of Death.* Tokyo: Tuttle Publishing, 2018.

Holbein, Hans. *Danse Macabre: The Dance of Death.* Montreal: Scriptoria, 2021.

Holland, Tom. "America Is Not Rome. It Just Thinks It Is," *The New York Review of Books*, August 6, 2019.

Homer, *The Illiad*, trans. Stanley Lombardo. New York: Hacket, 1997.

Honda, Katsuichi. [Main text from *Nankin e no Michi* (*The Road to Nanjing*), 1987.] *The Nanjing Massacre: A Japanese Journalist Confronts Japan's National Shame*, ed. Frank Gibney. M. E. Sharp, 1999.

Horace. *The Odes of Horace*, trans. David Ferry. New York: Farrar, Strauss, and Giroux, 1998.

"How Groups Voted in 2020," *Roper Center for Public Opinions Research*. Trump Won 58% of the White Vote in 2020.

Huang, Y., Z.Q. Chen, P.D. Roopnarine, M.J. Benton, L. Zhao, X. Feng, Z. Li. "The Stability and Collapse of Marine Ecosystems during the Permian-Triassic Mass Extinction," *Current Biology* 33(6), March 27, 2023: 1059–70.e4, doi: 10.1016/j.cub.2023.02.007. Epub 2023 Feb 24. PMID: 36841237.

The Hughes Brothers. *The Book of Eli.* Alcon Entertainment, 2010, 118 minutes.

Hurston, Zora Neal. *Their Eyes Were Watching God.* Harper Perennial, 1937.

Illing, Sean. "What America Can Learn from the Fall of the Roman Republic," *Vox*, January 1, 2019.

Ingram, David. "Facebook Goes Meta: Zuckerberg Announces New Corporate Name," *NBC News*, October 21, 2021.

James, Michael. "More than 1,000 in US Die in a Single Day from Coronavirus, Doubling the Worst Daily Death Toll of the Flu," *USA TODAY*, April 1, 2020.

Jameson, Frederic. "Future City," *New Left Review*, 2003.

Jameson, Leslie. "The Enduring Allure of Choose Your Own Adventure Books," *The New Yorker*, September 12, 2022.

Jamison, Leslie. *The Recovering: Intoxication and Its Aftermath.* New York: Little, Brown, 2018.

Jerome, "Letter 128,"

"John Clark's Latin Verse Machine: 19th Century Computational Creativity," *Electronic Literature Knowledge Base*, https://elmcip.net/critical-writing/john-clarks-latin-verse-machine-19th-century-computational-creativity.

Johnson, Alex, Andrew Blankstein and Alexandra Hess. "Three Dead, Suspect Killed in Shooting at Gilroy Garlic Festival in California," *NBC News*, July 29, 2019.

Jones, Emrys. *The New Oxford Book of Sixteenth Century Verse*. Oxford: Oxford University Press, 2009.

Judson, Anna P. "Eureka! It's an Automatic Latin Poetry Machine!" *It's All Greek to Me*, https://itsallgreektoanna.wordpress.com/2016/10/07/eureka-its-an-automatic-latin-poetry-machine/.

Kahn, Mattie. "How Instagram Turned a Holocaust Memoir into a Self-Help Manifesto," *Vox*, November 28, 2022.

Kaminsky, Ilya. *Deaf Republic: Poems*. Minneapolis, MN: Graywolf, 2019.

Kaplan, E. Ann. *Climate Trauma: Foreseeing the Future in Dystopian Film and Fiction*. New Brunswick, NJ: Rutgers University Press, 2015.

Kaplan, Seth. "'And I Knew Right Away': Could Mysterious Songbird Deaths in Pa. Be Connected to Cicadas?" *WHTM*, July 2, 2021.

Karl Capek, Karl. *R.U.R.*, trans. Claudia Novack-Jones. New York: Penguin, 2004, 21.

Kaup, Monika. *New Ecological Realisms: Post-Apocalyptic Fiction and Contemporary Theory*. Edinburgh: Edinburgh University Press, 2021.

Kelley, Stuart. *The Book of Lost Books: An Incomplete History of All the Great Books You'll Never Read*. London: Polygon, 2012.

Kelly, John. *The Great Mortality: An Intimate History of the Black Death*. New York: Harper Perennial, 2006.

King, Homay. *Virtual Memory: Time-Based Art and the Dream of Digitality*. Raleigh, NC: Duke University Press, 2015.

King, Stephen. *The Stand: Complete and Uncut Edition*. New York: Anchor, 2012.

Klingberg, Haddon. *When Life Calls Out to Us: The Love and Lifework of Viktor and Elly Frankl*. New York: Doubleday, 2001.

Kolbert, Elizabeth. *The Sixth Great Extinction: An Unnatural History*. New York: Henry Holt, 2014.

Krietzberg, Ian. "SpaceX Chief Elon Musk Explains What He Needs to Do to Colonize Mars," *TheStreet*, November 1, 2023.

Krugman, Paul. *The Great Unravelling: Losing Our Way in the New Century*. New York: W.W. Norton, 2004.

Kubis, Andy. "Researchers Trying to Figure Out What's Causing Mysterious Bird Deaths," *The Allegheny Front*, July 9, 2021.

Kushner, Tony. *Angels in America: A Gay Fantasia on National Themes: Revised and Complete Edition*. New York: Theater Communications Group, 2013.

Langer, Lawrence. "The Literature of Auschwitz," *Anatomy of the Auschwitz Death Camp*, ed. Yisrael Gutman and Michael Berenbaum. Bloomington, IN: Indiana University Press, in association with the United States Holocaust Memorial Museum, 1994.

Lawrence, D.H. *Studies in Classic American Literature*. New York: Thomas Selzer, 1928.

Laxer, Michael. "To the Veterans of the Abraham Lincoln Brigade," *The Left Chapter*.

Leavitt, David. *The Man Who Knew Too Much: Alan Turing and the Invention of the Computer*. New York: W.W. Norton, 2006.
Lerner, Sharon. "2.2 Million People in the U.S. Could Die if Coronavirus Goes Unchecked," *The Intercept*, March 17, 2020.
Levi, Primo. *The Periodic Table*. New York: Schocken Books, 1975.
Levinson, Jonathan, Conrad Wilson, James Doubek and Suzanne Nuyen. "Federal Offices Use Unmarked Vehicles to Grab People in Portland, DHS Confirms," *NPR*, July 17, 2020.
Lewis, Phillip. *The Public Humanities Turn: The University as an Instrument of Cultural Transformation*. Baltimore, MA: Johns Hopkins University Press, 2024.
Lincoln, Abraham. *The Gettysburg Address*, Gettysburg, PA, November 19, 1863.
Lincoln, Abraham. *The Lyceum Address*, Springfield, IL, January 27, 1838.
Lincoln, Abraham. "To Thomas Swann and Others," *Collected Works of Abraham Lincoln, Volume 7*. New Brunswick, NJ: Rutgers University Press, 1953.
Lombard, Maurice. "Urban Evolution in the Middle Ages," *From Internal Colonization in Medieval Europe*, ed. Felipe Fernandez-Armesto and James Muldoon. New York: Ashgate, 2008.
London, Jack. *The Scarlet Plague*. Orinda, CA: SeaWolf Press, 2018.
MacFarlane, Scott." Newly Obtained Video Shows Movement of Group Suspected of Constructing Jan. 6 Gallows Hours before Capitol Siege," *ABC News*, March 18, 2024.
Mailer, Norman. *The Naked and the Dead & Selected Letters 1945–1946*. New York: Library of America, 2023.
Mandel, Emily St John. *Station 11*. New York: Vintage, 2015.
Mann, Joshua. "Ohio Troops Halt Morgan's Raid at Battle of Buffington Island," *The Ohio Adjutant General's Office*.
Manseau, Peter and Jeff Sharlet. *Killing the Buddha: A Heretic's Bible*. New York: Free Press, 2004.
Marche, Stephen. "The College Essay Is Dead," *The Atlantic*, December 6, 2022.
Marche, Stephen. "The Computers Are Getting Better at Writing," *The New Yorker*, April 30, 2021.
Marcus, Greil. *The Shape of Things to Come: Prophecy and the American Voice*. New York: Faber and Faber, 2006.
Marsh, Linda. "Scorched Earth, 2200 A.D.," *Aeon*, February 10, 2015.
Mayor, Adrienne. *Gods and Robots: Myths, Machines, and Ancient Dreams of Technology*. Princeton, NJ: Princeton University Press, 2018.
McLaughlin, Elliot C. "Before January 6, Insurgents Waving Confederate Flags Hadn't Been within 6 Miles of the U.S. Capitol," *CNN*, January 7, 2021.
"Meeting with 90-Year-Old Holodomor Witness Mykola Onyshchenko," *Holodomor Museum*, December 10, 2024, https://holodomormuseum.org.

ua/en/news-museji/meeting-with-90-year-old-holodomor-witness-mykola-onyshchenko/.

Melin, Pia. *Fåfängans förgänglighet: allegorin som livs- och lärospegel hos Albertus Pictor*. Stockholm: Stockholmia, 2006.

Mikkelson, David. "Did This Photograph Appear on the El Paso Shooter's Twitter Page?" *Snopes*, August 3, 2019.

Milner, Andrew and J.R. Burgman. *Science Fiction and Climate Change: A Sociological Approach*. Liverpool: Liverpool University Press, 2020.

Montaigne, Michel de. *The Complete Essays*. New York: Penguin, 1993.

Moravec, Hans. *Mind Children: The Future of Robot and Human Intelligence*. Cambridge, MA: Harvard Belknap, 1988.

Motte, Jr., Warren F. *Oulipo: A Primer of Potential Literature*. Funks Grove, IL: Dalkey Archive Press, 2015.

Mueller, Benjamin and Eleanor Lutz. "U.S. Has Far Higher Covid Death Rate than Other Wealthy Countries," *The New York Times*, February 1, 2022.

Murphy, Cullen. "No, Really, Are We Rome?" *The Atlantic*, March 11, 2021.

"National Capital Columns," *U.S. National Arboretum*.

Nelson, Scott Reynolds. *Steel Drivin' Man: John Henry, the Untold Story of an American Legend*. Oxford: Oxford University Press, 2008.

Neuhasuer, Alan. "Donald Trump Jr., Ivanka Briefed on Russia Trump Tower Deal," *U.S. News and World Report*, February 27, 2019.

Neus, Nora. *24 Hours in Charlottesville: An Oral History of the Stand against White Supremacy*. Boston, MA: Beacon Press, 2023.

Newborn, Monty. *Kasparov versus Deep Blue: Computer Chess Comes of Age*. New York: Springer, 1996.

Now This, "Italian Opera Singer Serenades Quarantined Florence amidst Coronavirus Outbreak,"

Nyce, Caroline Mimbs. "QAnon Is a New American Religion," *The Atlantic*, May 14, 2020.

Obama, Barack. *Speech at the Democratic National Convention*, Boston, MA, July 27, 2004.

O'Connell, Mark. "Why Silicon Valley Billionaires Are Prepping for the Apocalypse in New Zealand," *The Guardian*, February 15, 2018.

O'Hara, Frank. *Meditations in an Emergency*. New York: Grove Press, 1957.

O'Kane, Caitlin. "Summer in the U.S. Could Be 8 Degrees Hotter in 2100—with Some Cities Feeling More Like the Middle East," *CBS News*, August 3, 2022.

Okri, Ben. "Artists Must Confront the Climate Crisis—We Must Write as if These Are the Last Days," *The Guardian*, November 12, 2021.

Oreskes, Naomi and Eric Conway. *The Collapse of Western Civilization: A View from the Future*. New York: Columbia University Press, 2014.

O'Toole, Fintan. "Donald Trump Had Destroyed the Country He Promised to Make Great Again," *The Irish Times*, April 25, 2020.

Packard, Edward. *The Cave of Time*. New York: Bantam, 1982.
Papazoglou, Alexis. "Is It Cruel to Have Kids in the Era of Climate Change?" *The New Republic*, February 25, 2019.
Papenfus, Mary. "As Far Right Violence Surges, Ted Cruz Seeks to Brand Antifa a Terrorist Organization," *Huffington Post*, July 21, 2019.
Perry, Eric. "Cashier Dead, Deputy Injured after Dispute with Man over a Mask, GBI Says," *FOX5 Atlanta*, June 14, 2021.
Peterson, Jordan. *12 Rules for Life: An Antidote to Chaos*. Toronto: Random House Canada, 2018.
Phillips, Kynala. "How HBO's 'Watchmen' Brought the 1921 Tulsa Race Massacre to Life," *The Wall Street Journal*, June 30, 2020.
Polantz, Katelyn. "January 6 Rioter 'QAnon Shaman' to Get His Headdress and Spear Back, Judge Rules," *CNN*, August 5, 2024.
Popper, Karl. *The Logic of Scientific Discovery*. London: Hutchingson, 1959.
Porter, Roy. *Flesh in the Age of Reason: The Modern Foundations of Body and Soul*. New York: W.W. Norton, 2005.
Queneau, Raymond. *Hundred Thousand Billion Poems*. Paris: Gallimard, 1962.
Racter. *The Policeman's Beard Is Half-Constructed*. New York: Grand Central Publication, 1984.
Regis, Edward. *Great Mambo Chicken and the Transhuman Condition: Science Slightly over the Edge*. New York: Basic Books, 1990.
Remarque, Erich Maria. *All Quiet on the Western Front*, trans. A.W. Wheen. New York: Ballantine, 1987.
Rennie, John. "The Immortal Ambitions of Ray Kurzweil: A Review of *Transcendent Man*," *Scientific American*, February 11, 2011.
Repucci, Sarah and Amy Slipowitz. "Democracy under Siege," *Freedom House*. Freedom in the World 2021: Democracy under Siege | Freedom House.
"Results of Lawsuits Regarding the 2020 Election," *Campaign Legal Center*.
Rigby, Kate. *Dancing with Disaster: Environmental Histories, Narratives, and Ethics for Perilous Times*. Charlottesville, VA: University of Virginia Press, 2015.
Ripatrazone, Nick. "Enormous Zippers Unfastening: Ten Poems for the End of the World," *The Millions*, April 8, 2016.
Rivera, Enrique. "William Shatner Experienced Profound Grief in Space. It Was the 'Overview Effect,'" *NPR*, October 23, 2022.
Rumi, Jalal al-Din. *The Essential Rumi*, trans. Coleman Banks. San Francisco, CA: Harper, 2004.
Sale, Kirkpatrick. *Rebels against the Future: Luddites and Their War on the Industrial Revolution*. New York: Basic Books, 1996.
Samet, Elizabeth D. *Soldier's Heart: Reading Literature through Peace and War at West Point*. New York: Farrar, Strauss and Giroux, 2004.

Sax, Boria. *Avian Illuminations: A Cultural History of Birds*. London: Reaktion Books, 2021.

Schneider, Nathan. "An Interview with Ann Neumann, Journalist of Death," *America: The Jesuit Review*, February 16, 2016.

Scranton, Roy William. *Learning to Die in the Anthropocene: Reflection on the End of Civilization*. San Francisco, CA: City Lights Publishers, 2015.

Scranton, Roy William. "We Broke the World," *The Baffler*, September 2019.

Scranton, Roy William. *We're Doomed. Now What: Essays on War and Climate Change*. New York: Soho, 2018.

Serenko, A. "The Great Resignation: The Great Knowledge Exodus or the Onset of the Great Knowledge Revolution?" *Journal of Knowledge Management* 27(4), 2023.

Shapiro, Fred R. "Who Wrote the Serenity Prayer?" *Yale Alumni Magazine*, July/August 2008.

Sharples, Mike. "John Clark's Latin Verse Machine: 19th Century Computational Creativity," *IEEE Annals of the History of Computing* 45(1), 2023.

Sharples, Mike and Rafael Perezy Perez. *Story Machines: How Computers Have Become Creative Writers*. London: Routledge, 2022.

Shea, Brendan. "Karl Popper: Philosophy of Science," *Internet Encyclopedia of Philosophy*, 2020.

Sheldrake, Martin. *Entangled Life: How Fungi Make Our World, Change Our Minds & Shape Our Futures*. New York: Random House.

Shelley, Mary. *The Last Man*. Oxford: Oxford University Press, 2008.

Shelley, Percy. *Collected Poems and Prose*. New York: Penguin, 2017.

Sheng, Zhang. *The Rape of Nanking: A Historical Study*. Berlin: Walter de Gruyter, 2021.

Sherman, William Tecumseh. Speech to the Michigan Military Academy, June 19, 1879.

Shilts, Randy. *And the Band Played On: Politics, People and the AIDS Epidemic*. New York: St. Martin's Press, 1987.

Silverman, Jerry. *Songs That Made History around the World*. New York: Mel Bay Publications, 1993.

Simon, Ed. "The Crucified God: A Death in Pictures," *The Marginalia Review of Books*, April 11, 2017.

Simon, Ed. *The Dove and the Dragon: A History of the Apocalypse*. Minneapolis, MN: Fortress, 2025.

Simon, Ed. "Ten Ways to Live Forever," *The Millions*, November 20, 2019.

Sloan, Allan. "The CARES Act Sent You a $1,200 Check but Gave Millionaires and Billionaires Far More," *ProPublica*, June 9, 2020.

Smith, Zadie. "Elegy for a Country's Seasons," *The New York Review of Books*, April 3, 2014.

Snyder, Timothy. *Bloodlands: Europe between Hitler and Stalin*. New York: Basic, 2016.

Snyder, Timothy D. *The Road to Unfreedom: Russia, Europe, America*. New York: Penguin Random House, 2018.

Solnit, Rebecca. *Hope in the Dark: Untold Histories, Wild Possibilities*. Chicago, IL: Haymarket, 2016.

Solomon, Andrew. *The Noonday Demon: An Atlas of Depression*. New York: Scribner, 2015.

Sontag, Susan. *Illness as Metaphor and AIDS and Its Metaphors*. New York: Picador, 2001.

Stevens, Wallace. *The Collected Poems of Wallace Stevens*. New York: Vintage, 2015.

Strauss, Steven. "8 Striking Parallels between the U.S. and the Roman Empire," *Salon*, December 26, 2012.

Subramanian, Meera. "Leap," *The World as We Know It: Dispatches from a Changing Climate*, ed. Amy Brady and Tajja Isen. New York: Catapult, 2022.

Sudbanthad, Pitchaya. "A Brief History of Breathing," *The World as We Know It: Dispatches from a Changing Climate*, ed. Amy Brady and Tajja Isen. New York: Catapult, 2022.

Sullivan, Becky. "Kyle Rittenhouse Is Acquitted of All Charges in the Trial over Killing 2 in Kenosha," *NPR*, November 19, 2021.

Sumner, Charles. "Freedom National, Slavery Sectional," Washington, DC, July 27, 1852.

"Survivor Testimonies, Memoirs, Diaries, and Letters," *The Holodomor Research and Education Consortium*.

Swift, Jonathan. *Gulliver's Travels*. New York: Penguin, 2003.

Swofford, Anthony. *Jarhead: A Marine's Chronicle of the Gulf War and Other Battles*. New York: Scribner, 2003.

Tacitus. *Histories, Books I-III*, trans. Clifford H. Morre. Cambridge, MA: Loeb Classical Library, 1925.

Tennyson, Alfred Lord. *Selected Poems*. New York: Penguin, 2008.

Terkel, Studs. *The Good War: An Oral History of World War II*. New York: The New Press, 2004.

Thompson, E.P. *The Making of the English Working Class*. New York: Vintage, 1966.

Torres, Ella. "Central Park Will Be the Site of a New Hospital for Coronavirus Patients," *ABC News*, March 31, 2020.

Trexler, Adam. *Anthropocene Fictions: The Novel in a Time of Climate Change*. Charlottesville, VA: University of Virginia Press, 2015.

Tripathy, Kumar P., Sourav Mukherjee, Ashok K. Mishra and A. Park Williams. "Climate Change Will Accelerate the High-End Risk of Compound Drought and Heatwave Events," *Publication of the National Academy of Sciences*, 2023.

Trumbo, Dalton. *Johnny Got His Gun*. New York: Bantam, 1984.
Twain, Mark. *The Adventures of Huckleberry Finn*. New York: Carles L. Webster, 1885.
Vermeulen, Pieter. *Literature and the Anthropocene*. London: Routledge, 2020.
Vidal, Gore. *United States Essays: 1952–1992*. New York: Broadway Books, 1993.
Virgil. *The Aeneid*, trans. Robert Fagles. New York: Penguin, 2008.
Vonnegut, Kurt. *Slaughterhouse-Five*. New York: Dial Press, 1999.
David Wallace-Wells, "The Uninhabitable Earth," *New York Magazine*, July 9, 2017.
Wallace-Wells, David. *The Uninhabitable Earth: Life after Warming*. New York: Crown, 2020.
Walter, George. *The Penguin Book of First World War Poetry*. New York: Penguin.
Wardrip-Fruin, Noah. "Christopher Strachey: The First Digital Artist?" *Grand Text Auto*. School of Engineering, University of California Santa Cruz, August 1, 2005.
Ware, Ben. "Nothing but the End to Come? Extinction Fragments," *e-flux*, 2020.
"Welcome to the World of the Polycrisis," *The Financial Times*.
Whitman, Walt. *The Complete Poems*. New York: Penguin, 2005.
Wiener, Anna. "What Is It about Peter Thiel?" *The New Yorker*, October 27, 2021.
Wilentz, Sean. "Who's Buried in the History Books?" *The New York Times*, May 24, 2011.
Willcock, S., G.S. Cooper, J. Addy *et al*. "Earlier Collapse of Anthropocene Ecosystems Driven by Multiple Faster and Noisier Drivers," *Nat Sustain* 6, 2023: 1331–42.
Williams, Julien. "DC's Biggest Landmarks, Ranked by How Frequently They're Destroyed in Hollywood Movies," *Thrillist*, September 1, 2016.
Williams, Penry. "Babington, Anthony (1561–1586)," *Oxford Dictionary of National Biography*. Oxford University Press, 2004.
Wilson, Dennis K. *Justice under Pressure: The Saint Albans Raid and Its Aftermath*. Lanham, MD: University Press of America, 2007.
Wilson, Robert O. "Background to the Crisis," *Center for Holocaust and Genocide Education, University of Northern Iowa*, December 10, 2024, https://chge.uni.edu/robert-wilson.
Winthrop, John. *A Model of Christian Charity*, 1630.
Wolf, Zachary B. "Dollars vs. Deaths Is the Sickening Choice Created by Coronavirus," *CNN Politics*, March 23, 2020.
Wolff, Martha Anne Wood. *The Master of the Playing Cards: An Early Engraver and His Relationship to Traditional Media*, 1979, Dissertation, Yale; UMI (ProQuest), Dissertation Services, 2002.
Wong, Matteo. "Artists Are Losing the War against AI," *The Atlantic*, October 2, 2023.

Wood, David. "On the Alleged Letters of Honorius to the Cities of Britain in 410," *La Revue Latomus*, September 2012.
World History Encyclopedia, "Thutmose III's Battle of Megiddo Inscription," https://www.worldhistory.org/article/1102/thutmose-iiis-battle-of-megiddo-inscription/.
Yudkowsky, Eliezer. Interview with Andrea Miotti. *Bankless*. Podcast transcript. February 23, 2023.
Yurchak, Alexei. *Everything Was Forever, until It Was No More: The Last Soviet Generation*. Princeton, NJ: Princeton University Press, 2006.
Zizek, Slavoj. *Living in the End Times*. New York: Verso, 2018.
Zuhl, Joanne. "How Trump Incites Violence: Understanding Stochastic Terrorism," *Street Roots*, August 9, 2019.

Index

Adler, Alfred 140
AIDS epidemic 25–7
Albrecht, Glenn 125
Alger, Horatio 10
The Allegheny Front 154
Anthropocene 8, 11–12, 123–51
apocalyptic/apocalypse 2–3, 6–7,
  9–15, 23, 28, 41, 44, 66, 74, 80,
  82, 85, 126, 130–1, 134–40,
  142, 144–7, 149, 151, 156–7,
  160, 162–4
Armageddon 2, 28, 64, 130, 135–6,
  163
Ars moriendi 116–17, 146
artificial intelligence (AI) 5, 92–3, 99
Atwood, Margaret, *The Handmaid's Tale* 81
Auden, W. H., *Collected Poems of Auden* 63–4, 163
authoritarianism 1–2, 5, 11, 30, 44,
  67, 74, 144, 161

Barnes, Julian, *Nothing to Be Frightened Of* 114–15
Bellot, Gabrielle 127–8
Benet, Stephen Vincent, "The Devil and Daniel Webster" 73
Bergman, Ingmar, *The Seventh Seal* 21, 112
Bezos, Jeff 108, 156

Biden, Joe 80
Black Death 19–21, 29–30
Blanchard, Arthur 97
Boccaccio, Giovani, *The Decameron* 21–2, 29, 35
Boethius 146–8
Boland, Eavan, *New Collected Poems* 43–4
Booth, Martin, *Hiroshima Joe* 55
Borges, Jorge Louis 94–5
Bouteldj, Ines 99
Bradshaw, Corey J. A., *Frontiers in Conservation Science* 6
Brady, Amy, *The World as We Knew It* 125
Brin, Sergey 108
Brooks, Max, *World War Z* 29
Burgman, J. R., *Science Fiction and Climate Change* 8
Burns, John, *The Gallery* 55
Bush, George W. 4, 10
Butler, Win, *The Suburbs* 3

calamity 11–12, 21, 147
Calhoun, John C. 79
Camus, Albert, *The Plague* 22
Capek, Karl, *R.U.R* 99–100
capitalist realism 9, 133–4
Capitol 39–40, 77–86, 153, 159
Carboniferous 124

Cavafy, Constantine 69, 86
Central Park 37–9, 45
Chang, Iris, *The Rape of Nanking* 50–1
Chat-GPT 3 5, 92–5, 99–103
Christianity 114–15, 136, 138
Civil War 38, 59, 61, 67, 78, 85, 159, 161
Clark, John 95–6
Clark, Timothy, *Ecocriticism on the Edge* 137–8
climate change 2, 4, 7, 11–13, 66, 126–7, 131–3, 135, 139, 150, 157, 161–2, 164
Club of Rome 7
Cohen, Leonard 74
Cole, Thomas, "The Course of Empire" 159–61
computers 5, 92–5, 97–8, 102, 111, 113–14, 116
Conway, Erik 147
creative existentialism 164
culture wars 147

DALL-E program 5, 92, 100
Dargan, Kyle, *Honest Engine: Poems* 102–3
Darwin, Charles, *Descent of Man, and Selection in Relation to Death* 154
death 31–2, 38, 40, 42–4, 52, 55, 57–60, 68, 70, 79, 105–14, 116–19, 124, 126, 132, 135–6, 146, 159
Debord, Guy, *Society of the Spectacle* 83
de Grey, Aubrey 107–9, 111
depression 32–4
Derrida, Jacques, *Diacritics* 136
Dickey, James 62
Doerries, Bryan, *The Theater of War* 57

El Akkad, Omar 126–8
Ellison, Ralph, *The Invisible Man* 73
Ellsworth, Elmer Ephraim 78
Emmanuel-Gobry, Pascal, "America now Looks like Rome before the Fall of the Republic" 160
Enzensberger, Hans Magnus 135
Eureka machine 95–7, 99

falsification principle 110, 116
fascism 10, 67, 80–1
Faulks, Sebastian, *The Vintage Book of War Fiction* 56
Febos, Melissa 127
feedback loops 6, 162
Fiedler, Leslie, *Love and Death in the American Novel* 85–6
Fisher, Mark, *Capitalist Realism* 9, 133–4
Fish, Stanley, *Is There a Text in this Class* 103
Fox, Nicols, *Against the Machine* 101–2
Frankl, Viktor, *Man's Search for Meaning* 139–45
Franzen, Jonathan 139
Freud, Sigmund 140
Fuqua, Antoine, *Olympus Has Fallen* 82
Fussell, Paul, *The Great War and Modern Memory* 61

Ghosh, Amitav, *The Great Derangement* 13
Gibbon, Edward, *The History of the Decline and Fall of the Roman Empire* 158, 162
gnosticism 115
Goldensohn, Lorrie, *American War Poetry* 61
Gourevitch, Philip, *We Regret to Inform You That Tomorrow*

We Will Be Killed with Our Families 62
Graeber, David, *Bullshit Jobs: A Theory* 102
Grant, Ulysses S. 81
Gray, John 115
Great Hunger 43
Great War 55–6, 60–2
Green, John, *The Anthropocene Reviewed* 12
Gross, Terry 119

Haines, Tasha, *Redemptive Hybridism in Post-Postmodern Writing* 13–14
Harjo, Laureate Joy 165
Harris, Kamala 80
Hassan, Naseer 138
Hatcher, John, *The Black Death* 21
Hedges, Chris, *War is a Force that Gives Us Meaning* 53
Heise, Ursula K., *Imagining Extinction* 130
Heller, Joseph, *Catch-22* 54
Hemingway, Ernest, *For Whom the Bell Tolls* 10, 57
Hemon, Aleksander, *The Book of My Lives* 62
Henry, John 89–90, 92, 95, 102
Herrington, Gaya 7
Hinojosa, Rolando 62
Holbein, Hans, *Danse Macabre* 30
Holland, Tom 161
Holodomor 52
Horace 11, 127–8
Huang, Yuangeng 6
humanity 8, 22, 51, 53, 57, 89, 100, 126, 129–30, 139–40, 147–9
hurricanes (Hurricane Sandy) 3, 6, 9, 65–6, 126, 129, 132, 139, 162
hypernormalization 8–10, 14

Isen, Tajja, *The World as We Knew It* 125

Jackson, Andrew 79
Jameson, Frederic 9, 131, 134

Kaplan, E. Ann, *Climate Trauma* 3
Kelly, John, *The Great Mortality* 19–20
Kennedy, John F. 82
King, Homay, *Virtual Memory* 98
Kingsnorth, Paul, Dark Mountain Project 131
King, Stephen, *The Stand* 27–8
Komunyakaa, Yusef 62
Krugman, Paul 4
Kubis, Andy 154
Kurzweil, Ray 107, 109, 111, 113, 115, 117–19
Kushner, Harold 143
Kushner, Tony, *Angels in America* 25–6, 143

Langer, Lawrence 142
Lawrence, D. H., *Studies in Classic American Literature* 71
Lee, Robert E. 77–8
LeGuin, Ursula K. 137, 164
Levi, Primo, *The Periodic Table* 124
Lewis, Phillip, *The Public Humanities Turn* 14
Lincoln, Abraham 38, 66–7, 72, 74, 78
Llull, Ramon, *Ars Magna* 94–5, 97
logotherapy 140–6
London, Jack, *The Scarlet Plague* 23–4

Mailer, Norman, *The Naked and the Dead* 54
Mandel, Emily St John, *Station Eleven* 23–4

Manseau, Peter, *Killing the Buddha* 44
Marche, Stephen 92, 99
Marcus, Greil, *The Shape of Things to Come* 72–3
Marsh, Linda 147
Mayor, Adrienne, *Gods and Robots* 90–1
Meade, George C. 78
Milner, Andrew., *Science Fiction and Climate Change* 8
Montaigne, Michel de 116
Moravec, Hans 114–15
Morgan, John Hunt 77
Musk, Elon 156

Neumann, Ann 107
New Curating 148–50
Niebuhr, Reinhold 143
9/11 38, 44, 82–3

Obama, Barack 10, 72–3
O'Brien, Tim, *The Things They Carried* 57
Okri, Ben 164
OpenAI 5
Oreskes, Naomi 147
O'Toole, Fintan 70
Owen, Wilfred 60–1

Packard, Edward, *The Cave of Time* 95
pandemic 2, 11, 19–30, 44, 67, 70, 126, 154–5, 162
Papazoglou, Alexis 139
Paris Agreement 6–7
Pax Americana 70
Perez y Perez, Rafael, *Story Machines* 93
pestilence 19–20, 22–3, 28, 30–5, 38, 40, 71
Peterson, Jordan 144

Pictor, Albertus 21
Platonism 115
polycrisis 4, 13, 15
Popper, Karl 110–11, 113, 116
Porter, Roy, *Flesh in the Age of Reason* 20
Prine, John 40
Putin, Vladimir 4

quarantine 22, 33–5, 39, 43
Queneau, Raymond, *Hundred Thousand Billion Poems* 95

Rabe, John, *Nanking Safety Zone* 51
Racter, *The Policeman's Beard is Half-Constructed* 98–9
Reagan, Ronald 26–7
Red Death (hemorrhagic fever) 23–4
Remarque, Erich Maria, *All Quiet on the Western* 54–5, 60
Rigby, Kate, *Dancing with Disaster* 22
robotics 92–3
Rothblatt, Martine 111–12

Sabeti, Arram 108
Sale, Kirkpatrick 102
Samet, Elizabeth D., *Soldier's Heart* 57
Sandingham, John (character) 55
Sassoon, Siegfried 60–1
Sax, Borian, *Avian Illuminations* 155
Scranton, Roy, *We're Doomed. Now What?* 129–38, 148
Sebastian, Saint, Master of the Playing Cards 19–20
Second World War 56, 62, 75
Sendak, Maurice 119
Sharlet, Jeff, *Killing the Buddha* 44
Sharples, Mike, *Story Machines* 93
Shelley, Mary, *The Last Man* 24–5
Sherman, William Tecumseh 54

Shilts, Randy, *And the Band Played On* 26–7
Shovkovytsia, Petro 52
Smith, James 23
Smith, Zadie, "Elegy for a Country's Seasons" 150
Snyder, Timothy D.
  Bloodlands 53
  The Road to Unfreedom 4
solastagia 125
Solnit, Rebecca, *Hope in the Dark* 164
Solomon, Andrew, *The Noonday Demon* 33–5
Sontag, Susan, *Illness as Metaphor* 28–30
Stalin, Joseph 51–2
Stevens, Wallace 149
Strachey, Christopher 98
Subramanian, Meera 128–9
Sudbanthad, Pitchaya 125
Swift, Jonathan, *Gulliver's Travels* 94–6
Swofford, Anthony, *Jarhead* 62–3

Taggard, Genevieve 74
Teasdale, Sarah 62
Tennyson, Alfred Lord, *Selected Poems* 58–60
Terkel, Studs, *The Good War* 62
Thiel, Peter 108, 112–14, 116–17, 156
Thompson, E. P., *The Making of the English Working Class* 101
Tichborne, Chidiock 105–9, 114, 118
Tokyo Nichi Nichi Shimbun 49
Tolkien, J. R. R., *Lord of the Rings* 28
tragic optimism 142
transhumanism 113–17
Trexler, Adam, *Anthropocene Fictions* 126

Tripathy, Kumar P. 6
Trooze, Adam 4
Trumbo, Dalton, *Johnny Got His Gun* 54
Trumbull, John 81
Trump, Donald 10, 73, 81, 85
Turing, Alan 97–8
Twain, Mark, *The Adventures of Huckleberry Finn* 73

verification principle 110
Vermeulen, Pieter, *Literature and the Anthropocene* 125
Vidal, Gore, *United States Essays* 159
Virgil, *The Aeneid* 56
von Clausewitz, Carl, *On War* 53–4
Vonnegut, Kurt, *Slaughterhouse-Five* 54

Wallace-Wells, David, *The Uninhabitable Earth* 6–7, 10, 139, 161–2
war 39, 49–64, 67, 91, 100–2, 141, 148, 150
Ware, Ben 11
Whitman, Walt, *The Complete Poems* 58–60
Wilson, Robert O. 50
Winthrop, John 72

Yudkowsky, Eliezer 5
Yurchak, Alexei, *Everything Was Forever, Until It Was No More* 8–9

ZeroCater 108
Žižek, Slavoj, *Living in the End Times* 156